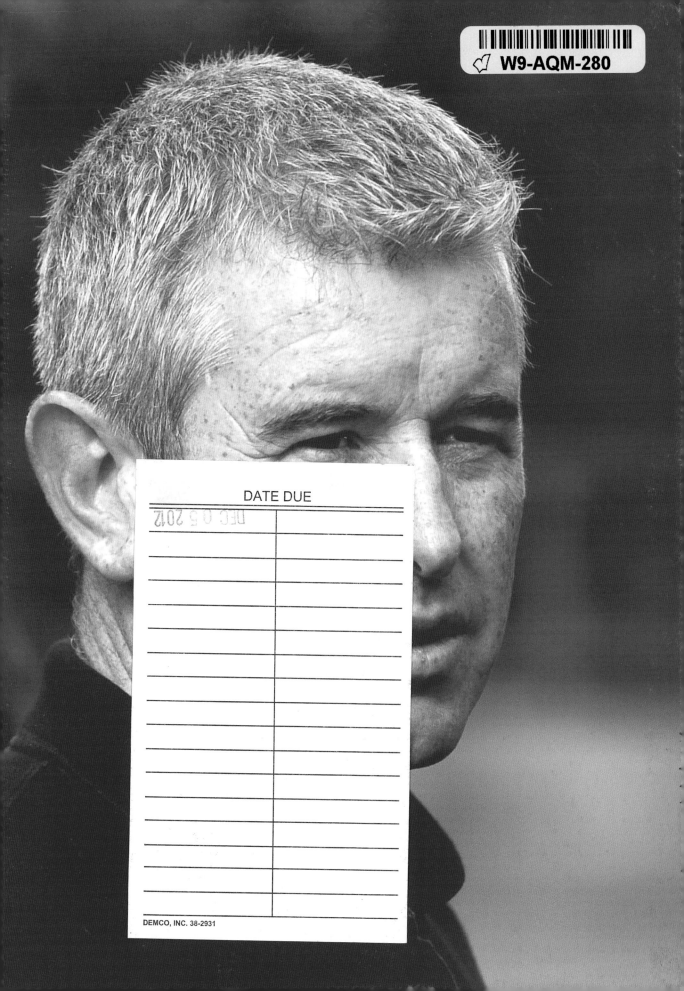

DATE DUE

Richard Maxwell

MAXIMIZE YOUR
HORSEMANSHIP

FIND THE EXCELLENCE IN YOU
AND YOUR HORSE

D&C
David and Charles

A DAVID & CHARLES BOOK

Copyright © David & Charles Limited 2006

David & Charles is an F+W Publications Inc. company
4700 East Galbraith Road
Cincinnati, OH 45236

First published in the UK in 2006

Text copyright © Richard Maxwell 2006
Photographs copyright © David & Charles 2006, except page 101 copyright ©
    Horsepower Photography at www.horsepower-photography.com
Photography by Matthew Roberts except page 101 (see above for details)

ISBN-13: 978-0-7153-2408-0 hardback
ISBN-10: 0-7153-2408-X hardback

Printed in China by R.R. Donnelley
for David & Charles
Brunel House   Newton Abbot   Devon

Commissioning Editor Jane Trollope
Editor Jennifer Proverbs
Designers Sue Cleave and Charley Bailey
Production Beverley Richardson
Text Editor Johanna Legh-Smith

Visit our website at www.davidandcharles.co.uk

David & Charles books are available from all good bookshops; alternatively you
can contact our Orderline on 0870 9908222 or write to us at FREEPOST EX2 110,
D&C Direct, Newton Abbot, TQ12 4ZZ (no stamp required UK only); US customers
call 800-289-0963 and Canadian customers call 800-840-5220.

Contents

Introduction

I've been working with horses of all shapes, sizes and temperaments for over 20 years now, and each one of them has contributed to this book in their own way.

Some of my equine clients have had serious behavioural difficulties that took every ounce of my mind and body power to resolve; others were more straightforward personalities whose full potential was compromised by poor communication or a minor misunderstanding.

As I got better at reading what the horse was trying to tell me, I also became aware of how, by changing the small things, the bigger problems started to sort themselves out, and that by having the basics in place the overall improvement was huge. The basics that I'm talking about are things that probably don't even cross our minds, such as backing up, which is such a crucial part of how your horse views you as a person and rider. By starting to perfect backing up, in hand, then in the saddle, you will totally change the dynamics of your relationship. The basics form the foundations of what I now call the training pyramid.

After a conventional start to my riding and teaching career, I became more and more fascinated with exploring the horse's mind, rather than just studying how he used his body when working. The influence of the horse's psyche on his training and performance was a crucial area of knowledge that I had barely touched on until then, and this realization has led to the development of the methods outlined in this book. They form the core of the most effective and humane training process I have yet come across, which is why I use them. However huge the talent of horse and/or rider, it means nothing unless it can be trained into a consistently usable form.

Natural horsemanship techniques are now increasingly familiar to the horse owner, and are widely acknowledged and accepted by the equine industry. But we still have a long way to go, and I continue to see many promising partnerships at best under-achieve and at worst completely crumble through lack of a true understanding of how to train a horse. Learning to ride a horse is *not* the same as learning to train one. This book aims to build on your current riding skills to help you become an effective and sympathetic trainer of horses. As always, our best teachers are the horses themselves, and I hope this book will help you to learn from their lessons.

Those who have read my previous book *Unlock Your Horse's Talent* (David & Charles, 2003) may find some of the techniques familiar, but I promise that any repetition is kept to a minimum and will only appear when absolutely necessary. In any case, repetition is a useful way to jog memory. Training horses is all about repetition; the more successful repetitions you have, the more solid the training.

My aim throughout is to help anyone who owns a horse to enjoy him to the maximum, whatever their goals. Whether you simply want to hack out safely or hope to compete successfully at a high level, I can give you the tools to do it and will be sharing my own personal stories, mistakes and achievements along the way.

Richard Maxwell

MAXIMIZE YOUR HORSEMANSHIP

So how does this book help me to maximize my horsemanship?

Chapter 1: AIMS AND PRINCIPLES

Why you need more than your current riding skills to become an effective trainer of horses; setting standards and creating a bond with your horse; the importance of groundwork for the ridden horse; ten vital training principles; how to plan a schooling schedule using the training pyramid, a system for every horse and rider, whatever their goals

Chapter 2: THE TRAINING MINDSET

The principles that make a good trainer, and some basic rules to form the core of your 'good training handbook', such as assessing your own current skill levels; setting up non-negotiable ground rules; how horses learn and how to use this to your advantage; why you need respect for and from your horse; the principles of correction; the role of physical, mental and emotional wellbeing in creating a trainable horse

Chapter 3: BUILDING THE FOUNDATIONS

The fundamental elements that make up a training plan or pyramid; establishing good groundwork using a training halter, rope circling and long lines; the benefits of a firm training base; improving your skills

Chapter 4: IMPROVING AND USING YOUR NEW SKILLS

Using groundwork to improve ridden performance; how the horse's brain works; exercises to help him learn; how to keep his focus and attention even in challenging situations; focus control; concludes with a useful Question-and-Answer section

Chapter 5: PROGRESS, PROBLEMS AND SOLUTIONS

The development of strength, balance and co-ordination to produce a consistently good ridden performance; key exercises for improvement and problem solving; fine-tuning your horse's performance; reaching the top of the pyramid

CASE STUDIES

Real-life examples of the techniques at work are included throughout the book

Chapter 1
AIMS AND PRINCIPLES

Many of us are not entirely happy with our horse or horses. Some people may have a serious ridden problem, but more often it is just that the horse regularly does something that they don't like, but think they can't change, such as not standing still, head butting, spooking when out hacking and generally lacking focus on the rider. To be successful at training or re-training your horse, I believe you need to have a good idea of what you want to achieve and to know some of the underlying elements that are key to good training. In this chapter I explain how making small changes, both physically and mentally, can make a huge impact on your relationship with your horse and on his performance. I also outline the principles behind my training system and how to use these in formulating your own system .

I've already mentioned Unlock Your Horse's Talent *(David & Charles, 2003); a very practical book that describes all my techniques.* Maximize Your Horsemanship *is not strictly a 'how-to' book, it aims to describe the training mindset, which involves thinking about why horses and humans behave as they do. By understanding the psychology of learning and training, you can get closer to achieving whatever horsemanship aims you have. However, as we are now very visual learners, I have made a DVD showing all the groundwork and long-lining techniques. It is contains around four hours of footage and is available through www.richard-maxwell.com.*

Great expectations

So, first of all, do you need to read this book?

Your horse is great. No problems at all. Well… he won't always stand for the farrier, hates leaving the yard without his mates, won't always load at shows and barges you out of the way at feed time, but apart from that… he's just great!

It never ceases to amaze me how much rude behaviour people will tolerate from their horses. Problems like those listed above are so common as to be considered almost normal. But why do we accept them? What makes us think we have to settle for less-than-perfect manners? How do we become brainwashed into restricting our equine goals and dreams to the mundane, and thinking that we (or our horses) 'can't' or 'shouldn't' do something? Of course, you don't want to overface the horse, but if you've owned him for years and are still trotting around in never-ending 20-metre circles, there is something amiss with your training programme.

No more excuses. A high level of understanding, respect and co-operation is within the reach of every rider on any horse, so long as they are prepared to follow a logical, progressive system. What's more, correct schooling is highly beneficial for the horse and fun for the rider, whether you plan to compete or not. You owe it to your horse to ensure he is using his mind and body correctly, not just under saddle but in every interaction you have with him: on the ground or under saddle, in the arena or stable yard, at home or away.

Even if you've never trained a horse in your life, it doesn't mean you can't, provided you are prepared to dedicate yourself to a logical, progressive and sympathetic training programme like the one outlined in this book. If you are willing to dedicate your time and energy to making some changes, then I can help you achieve things with your horse you didn't think were possible – and you can do it without losing that bond you have formed and the trust that is already in place.

If you haven't yet formed a bond or you feel that the trust between you and your horse isn't quite as you would like, following this basic structure will soon put you back on track. If you are worried that your riding isn't up to problem solving or you have lost your confidence with a particular horse, never fear as we'll be spending a lot of time out of the saddle anyway, starting with essential groundwork to allow you to analyse the problem objectively and take charge of the situation.

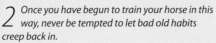

*No more excuses.
Even if you've never trained
a horse in your life,
it doesn't mean you can't*

1 *Even when you are working around your horse on the yard, he should be respectful of your personal space.*

2 *Once you have begun to train your horse in this way, never be tempted to let bad old habits creep back in.*

3 *Using the principles outlined in this book has allowed me to event and to have a horse that is willing and enjoys his job.*

4 *Loose jumping is a great way to add variety to your work programme, even if you don't jump when riding.*

5 *These principles are not about getting rid of personality. Mattie is expressing himself but in a controlled environment.*

Groundwork?
But I want to ride!

The overall plan is to help you make your horse safer to be around, to handle and, most importantly, to ride. It is well known that I have always used a lot of ground training in the work I do, but my experiences over the last three years have really emphasized to me how important it is.

Quite simply, working from the ground will solve a high percentage of ridden problems, without confusing the horse or putting the rider's confidence at risk. When combined with ridden work, it will cement your relationship with your horse, no matter what level you are at. It also adds variety to your schooling and improves your skills, timing and feel. So I won't apologize for going over the groundwork because the fact is, it's an absolutely essential part of laying down good foundations and enabling you to have a horse that you can enjoy.

Once you have got to grips with the groundwork, we will look at how it can improve your everyday riding, whether your interest is hacking, jumping or dressage. If you have more serious problems to deal with, such as bucking, rearing and napping, it can help with these too. By developing good groundwork skills you will have the tools to deal with anything that the horse throws at you, whether in hand or ridden, and will soon become much more than just his rider: you'll become his trainer.

By developing good groundwork skills you will have the tools to deal with everything that the horse throws as you …
and will soon become much more than just his rider:
you'll become his trainer

MAXIMIZE YOUR HORSEMANSHIP

The value of groundwork

For some time, something had been really bothering me. Although I was progressing well with horses that came in to be started, and those that had ridden or handling problems, I didn't seem to making much headway with those niggling schooling issues that undermine performance but are a long way from what could be called full-blown ridden problems. All riders have them, after all, while very few have true ridden problems.

So what could I do to tackle them and improve the performance of the horses I was working with? Years after watching an amazing demonstration by one of the original American natural horsemen, Ray Hunt, it was all about to fall into place for me. Quite by accident I was about to make the connection between groundwork and ridden work.

I owned a horse that was not improving in his ridden work at all. I was so frustrated that, to allow myself thinking time, I got off his back and started to work him from the ground, alternating the two main components of ground training: halter work and long-lining. After about two months of this, I thought I would get back on my horse and see if I could get any inspiration. I was completely amazed at the result. With no ridden work at all, my horse had become light, soft, engaged and obedient to the aids! Working without a rider to hold him up (photograph left) had

taught him self-balance. Of course, he wasn't perfect all of the time, but the improvement was enormous, and at last I had some effective tools in place that enabled me to correct problems as they cropped up.

Whenever I get a new horse now, I start by doing 80 per cent groundwork and 20 per cent ridden; over two to three months I reverse that to 80 per cent ridden and 20 per cent groundwork, but groundwork definitely becomes part of the whole schooling process forever.

A tale of two trainers

Scattered through the book you will find some case studies that illustrate how my training techniques apply to the lives of real-life riders. Two of them are from teenage boys, one an event rider and the other a show jumper, both of whom are successful in their chosen discipline. With both boys I went through a similar training programme, and both have done well, but one of them definitely made better progress than the other in the early stages. When I read their case studies, I was able to see why. I would like to make it clear right now that I am not criticizing either of them; after all, they had the foresight to recognize they had a problem that needed sorting and to call me out in the first place. I just found the contrast in their reports fascinating.

The first case study was from the show jumper (see pages 64–5). What came out of his report was that he didn't really see the value of ground training, but that he would use it as a last resort if his horse got really bad. It definitely wasn't part of his daily training programme. He is a lovely lad and I only hope that as he gets older he will see the benefit of ground training, and realize that it is not just for emergencies, but is the vital key to progress and a more consistent performance.

The second report was from the event rider who at first thought I was a complete idiot (see pages 110–11). It was his mum who wanted me to come and help out. Once I arrived, however, it didn't take him long to see the value of the ground training and to implement it in his daily schooling plan. The difference it made to his very difficult pony was huge, and he went from struggling to get through an event to being consistently successful. If he continues to use all that he has learnt with every horse he rides, he will be able to maintain this success, because all his horses will become so responsive and respectful that he will then be able to get much more out of them through willingness and trust.

Whether your ultimate goal is to compete at any level or just hack out safely, establishing the basics will pay dividends. Often it does involve going back and cementing the basics, but you will reap the rewards.

For me, ground training is the key to having a successful working relationship, both in the stable and under saddle. **It is the vital key to progress.**

12345
Planning and preparation

Before you get your horse out and head for the school, you must first understand these ten principles. They are the key to developing a better relationship with your horse, and you must abide by them faithfully if you are to become a successful trainer.

The title of this section is my father-in-law's favourite saying! No matter what he is doing, the planning and preparation that go into it are meticulous. It used to be a family joke, but actually he always achieves his end goal with ease and within target, whether it is a time target or a financial one. Perhaps his military background has something to do with it, but even though I am an ex-soldier, I have always been a bit haphazard.

My saying used to be 'I'll get there in the end', but nobody knew when that end would be, not even me! This has all changed since I started using what I call a 'training pyramid' to give structure and order to every horse's training programme. The concept of a training pyramid is central to the way I train horses, and you'll read a lot more about it in the following chapters. Basically, it entails making sure a broad training base is firmly in place, to support the more advanced and complex work at the pinnacle of the pyramid.

As a result of incorporating the training pyramid, I am achieving so much more within my life and within my relationship with my horses, every day as well as in competition. The message is that you must have a plan with easily achievable targets if you are to enjoy that all-important motivating factor, progress. Without a structure, your training is unlikely to lead to your goal, whatever that might be. So whether you have a daily or weekly plan, make one to ensure that you get the most out of your time with your horse.

*The message is that you must have a plan with easily achievable targets if you are to enjoy that all-important motivating factor…***progress**

prevent poor performance

Plan ahead. If you know you want to do some 'spook' work, set up the arena beforehand so everything is ready for your session.

Understand the value of

To some degree everything we do with our horses involves pressure, but I have found that 'pressure' can be misunderstood as force. Knowing the value of pressure will improve your relationship with your horse, whether on the ground or in the saddle.

Pressure is a marker that we use to help the horse to understand the difference between right and wrong. This basically translates into the horse choosing to stay in a comfort zone (where he is doing the right thing, so pressure is released) or a discomfort zone (where continued pressure indicates to the horse that he is doing the wrong thing).

There is a often a misconception about pressure, probably because we humanize it. To us, pressure equals stress, whereas when used correctly the horse can perceive it as a fair and normal way of communicating. Pressure is only unfair when it is excessive, when it is forcing the horse to do something he cannot comfortably achieve either physically or mentally, or when there is no release for a correct response.

Whatever form it takes, never think of the pressure you use as punishment or force; in the early days any pressure you apply may be very obvious, but as your horse learns to respond more quickly, it will become so subtle you'll hardly feel it. (For more about pressure and release, see page 58.)

The second Mattie makes a forward movement, the pressure comes off. His ears indicate he is focusing on what I am asking. Remember to reward the smallest effort.

pressure

Pressure is a marker *that we use to help the horse to understand the difference between right and wrong*

Praise each positive action,

If you think about what motivates you within life and the work place, then this will give you an idea of when and how to praise your horse. At the end of a working day, would you rather be told by your boss that you have done a great job and thanked for it, or perhaps that you are doing a great job but there are a few areas that could be improved upon? Or would you rather your boss didn't say anything about whether you were doing well or not until annual appraisal time?

Most people find it far more motivating to be told that they are doing well on a regular basis, or to have small areas where they could improve pointed out to them, so that they can choose to do something about them before things reach crisis point. It's good to know you are doing the right thing and achieving what is expected of you.

If you had to wait a whole year for feedback on your performance, by the time it came you probably wouldn't care one way or the other. You would have long since become demotivated, especially if you were only pulled up when something was going wrong and the feedback was purely negative.

So when you are training your horse, remember to praise every positive action, however small. Don't wait until the final result is achieved; praise every effort your horse makes in the right direction. For example, when I am loading a difficult horse, I don't wait until the horse is in the trailer with the ramp up before I praise him. I praise him for every forward-thinking movement he makes; remember in the early days it is about rewarding the horse for trying, not necessarily succeeding all the way, so even a step or a sway in the right direction needs to be praised.

If you had to wait a whole year for feedback on your performance, by the time it came you probably wouldn't care one way or the other.

however small

'Praise' doesn't mean a big hug and a handful of treats, just a small release of the pressure and maybe a rub between the eyes is sufficient. Be careful only to use praise for a job well done however; it must not be used as encouragement, since if your horse then fails in the task set, he has been rewarded for failing. Tell him he is a 'good boy' only when he has actually done something positive, not when he is still thinking about it or is simply standing there minding his own business and ignoring you!

12345

Be firm but fair

Horses respect:
firmness *not aggression,*
empathy *not sentiment,*
consistency *not inflexibility,*
persistence *not nagging.*

Being firm enough, without resorting to aggression, is one of the hardest things to teach people, especially as many horse owners love their horse and want him to love them back. When it comes to training your horse, it takes an equal measure of firmness and fairness to be successful. One doesn't work without the other, and getting the balance right is the key to gaining respect. This principle applies to all areas of horse ownership, not just riding and training. Do not confuse respecting someone with liking them; I have liked many of my teachers, but have respected only a few. At the other end of the scale, aggression creates fear and panic in the horse, and all he will want to do is run away. Fear causes horses (and people for that matter) to shut down mentally and become incapable of learning.

Getting your horse's respect without creating fear is easier than you think. All it takes is a simple understanding of a horse's natural instincts, so that you know what governs his behaviour and can then make allowances for it. In a herd situation, the leader has the ability to control the movement and direction of the other horses. When she (it's usually a mare) decides that the herd will move off to water or a new pasture, she goes and the rest will follow. If a mare wants to control a foal at foot she does so by using forms of tactile and visual pressure to get the foal to move its feet, look at her and to follow. She is firm but fair; the mare and her foal have a strong and loving bond, but the mare is still in charge without creating fear or suffering any loss of respect.

In the early part of our lesson Ferdi really questioned my requests. He was used to doing it all his own way, and wanted this to continue. However, by remaining firm, but fair in my expectations, I convinced him to try for me.

1 2 3 4 5

Ask clearly and precisely

At the end of a schooling session, how often have you been more exhausted than your horse, with shoulders aching from holding him up and legs numb from constantly asking for more impulsion?

Problems in horse behaviour frequently stem from confusion about what the handler actually wants. If the horse becomes confused about what is required, he will either ignore the rider/handler, or become agitated. This often leads to a much harsher request from the rider/handler because they are frustrated at what they perceive to be a lack of response.

You only have to look at your own life to understand how frustrating it is if someone gives you a task or job that they haven't explained very well. There is nothing worse than that 'I don't know what I'm supposed to be doing' feeling, and often you'll either switch off or become agitated. Either way, the task will end up taking far more effort than necessary.

It's true that we must be responsible for our own actions, but we also have to hand over some of the initiative to the horse and give him responsibilities too. This is a hard thing to do as we have been conditioned into micro-managing our horses; we want to support them in all their failings.

We have to get into the habit of giving precise instructions in the first place, then letting our horses learn by their mistakes and work out what is needed.

I hold out my arm to the side, so that Mattie can see clearly which direction I am asking him to go in.

Less is more

Sometimes doing nothing is the hardest thing in the world!

For me, less is definitely more when it comes to schooling horses. I like to be able to ask them to move away from my leg and allow them to do just that until I change the instruction. I do not expect to have to constantly suggest with my legs that I want forward movement. Likewise, when working a horse on the bit, I expect to ask my horse politely to come down on the bit and stay there. This approach is not just better for your horse, it is nicer for you, too. Do you want to turn into the type of rider who is constantly nagging with his legs, fiddling with the reins and nodding his head in an effort to do all the work for his horse? Thought not! Not only would you be exhausted, but the horse would soon switch off. Nobody likes to be nagged.

Watch a professional rider. They hardly seem to do anything when they are on their horse, which is just as well, as you can imagine how tiring it would be to ride several horses a day and constantly have to use your hands, legs and seat to such a degree. It's also very demoralizing for the horse. Can you imagine how you would feel if your boss asked you to type something, and then stood by your shoulder continually repeating this request until you had finished the work? Credit your horse with a little more intelligence and give him the opportunity to do the right thing, which in turn gives you the opportunity to either praise or correct him. How else will he learn?

Don't forget, sustained pressure without release causes stress, *which inhibits learning. There must be release for your horse to learn.*

When I am working horses my aim is to get more by doing less – here I am asking Jo to do a turn on the quarters without using reins.

My Top 10 Training Principles

Make the right thing easy

The main training principle in this book and in the way I work with horses is the use of pressure and release. In other words, when the horse isn't doing as asked I place him in an uncomfortable position both physically and emotionally, and he is under pressure. As soon as he does the right thing, the pressure is immediately taken off, so he learns the value of behaving correctly.

Timing is crucial if the horse is to associate his correct behaviour with the release of pressure. For example, if you have a horse that won't load into a trailer, you have to make his decision to stay outside the trailer uncomfortable. He must learn that although he is free to make his own decisions, there will be consequences if he chooses to behave negatively. In exactly the same way, there are consequences if he decides to behave positively – nice consequences, that is! As soon as he decides to come into the trailer, it becomes the best place in the world to be. All pressure is off and he gets lots of praise.

Even if the horse then decides to leave the trailer uninvited, no pressure must be put on him until he is actually outside the trailer. It doesn't take a horse long to work out that he can make himself more comfortable by doing the right thing. Meanwhile, as a sympathetic trainer, you are busy setting up a situation that makes doing the right thing easy for him. It's called creating a win-win situation.

It doesn't take a horse long to work out that it's easier for him to do the right thing.

Long-lining has been hugely beneficial in helping Jo carry himself. Here he is not relying on the lines to prop him up.

Say what you mean and mean what you say

How many times have you heard a parent say to a child in the shops, a restaurant or at the park 'If you do that again, we are going home'? Yet how many parents do you see carry out that threat when the child repeats the behaviour? Very few in my experience, and so the child learns that threats are empty and that there aren't really any consequences to bad behaviour.

If you are going to make a threat, make one that's easy for you to carry out. For example, a parent in that situation would be better saying that the child won't be allowed to have ice cream or watch television when they get home, provided of course that they stick to it.

So how does this relate to you and your horse? It's about not giving in when it gets a bit tough or embarrassing, which is what happens so often with the parents of that naughty child. If you have a horse that doesn't stand while he is being mounted and you have decided that you are going to retrain his behaviour, then that is what you must do. If you start the task and after ten minutes your horse is still not standing, it's too easy to say you will try again another day. Another day it will take even longer, because you have taught your horse that you don't mean what you say.

This situation usually arises because people don't know how to communicate what they want to the horse, and don't have a plan of how they intend to tackle a particular issue. Remember that 'planning and preparation prevent poor performance' so you might need to do some research beforehand, allow plenty of time, seek assistance if necessary and set up an environment that is conducive to success, such as having the arena free of other people and hazards, the mounting block ready or the trailer parked in a safe place. You must know exactly what you want and how to ask, then stick at it until you succeed (see point 10, pages 32–3).

> *However hard you find it to be assertive, **it's crucial** for your horse's understanding to say what you mean and mean what you say.*

Ferdi is a very clever horse and has taught everyone around him exactly how he likes things to be done; as long as they comply, he coasts along. Here, I had asked a question that he didn't like. I was fair in what I asked, so I didn't allow his behaviour to change the question. Eventually he realized I meant what I said and he then went beautifully.

My Top 10
Training Principles

Don't let thinking time become an excuse for your horse to lose his focus and attention. Mattie has been distracted (above), so he will be put back to work.

Once I have schooled a horse to respond to a training halter (above), I will move on to using a 'horseman's' halter (right).

8 9 10

Allow your horse thinking time

The importance of thinking time is something that very few trainers appreciate, and hardly any horses get enough of it.

It is so easy to keep going when things are going well and not allow the horse time to think about what has just happened. Horses react much faster than humans, but think more slowly, so you really do need to allow for this and give them that thinking time.

Thinking time must always follow a period of pressure. When your horse responds and gives to the pressure, he isn't able to analyse straightaway why the pressure was taken off, so he needs time to think about it afterwards. I find it takes most horses around three attempts to 'get it'. If you were to release the pressure and then re-apply it straightaway, the horse is unable to learn what it was he did to achieve the release, which will therefore compromise your progress. This applies to ridden work, too.

A quick example would be a horse that doesn't like to stand to be mounted and walks away as soon as the rider is on. Once these basic issues are sorted out, it is too easy to regress to hopping on board and immediately letting the horse walk off. To make sure the results are more long term, get in the habit of allowing the horse to stand for a few moments before asking him to walk off, to prevent the problem recurring.

When I am working with bad loaders, the thinking time is vital. I really can see them working things out, and standing in front of hundreds of horses with loading problems for a few hours at a time and observing their behaviour has taught me a lot over the years. The biggest factor for success is allowing them the time to reflect on their behaviour and its consequences. It is vital to progressive training.

Thinking time must always follow a period of pressure.

My Top 10 Training Principles

Sarah and Dan jump happily through water. Whether it's teaching your horse to lead nicely or jump through water, you need to make sure you succeed in your task. We hired a cross-country course and gave ourselves all day to achieve this result but it only took 30 minutes.

Don't start something you can't finish

This goes hand-in-hand with point eight, which is to say what you mean and mean what you say. We've talked about having a plan; now make sure that you are realistic about the time it will take to carry out that plan.

Choose a day when you haven't got to be somewhere, so that in your mind you are completely relaxed about the fact that you have all day to complete your task. If you start the task with two hours to sort something out, you will generally fail before you have even begun. You will be clock-watching from the start and your whole demeanour will tell the horse that you are under pressure, putting you at an immediate disadvantage.

Horses are expert observers of mood and readers of body language. If you think you really know what your horse is telling you, **remember that he knows you even better!**

With the TOP 10 PRINCIPLES established, I'll show you how to construct your **TRAINING PYRAMID**

Making a plan

Now you have all those principles firmly in mind, let's make a plan. The concept of a training pyramid has completely changed my approach to life, and when it comes to training horses, it is central to developing a logical training system that is built on solid foundations. Think of the shape of a pyramid, with the broad base supporting an

The Pyramid Plan

LEVEL 4

Advancing towards your goal

HALF-HALT

LEVEL 3

These are the components to a horse 'going on the bit'

SUPPLENESS

RHYTHM

LEVEL 2

Dextrous and obedient – both physically and mentally

REIN-BACK & CONTROL OF BACKWARD MOVEMENT

TURN ON THE FOREHAND

LEVEL 1

Pleasant and polite horse

ABILITY TO MOVE FEET IN ALL DIRECTIONS

MOVES OFF PRESSURE IN ALL DIRECTIONS

TRUST & RESPEC

ever-narrowing structure up to the pinnacle. For me, this image provides the ideal schooling plan. The first two levels are universal, regardless of your goal – from hacking to competing. If your goal is to achieve a safe horse to hack out, then that goal will sit on top of the first two levels. The third level builds on key skills and starts you on the road to competition success, while the fourth level deals with fine-tuning. Then, there you are – at the top!

THE PINNACLE

PACES WITHIN A PACE

SHORTENING & LENGTHENING

NGAGEMENT

STRAIGHTNESS

SELF-CARRIAGE

TURN ON THE QUARTERS

LATERAL MOVEMENT: SHOULDER-IN

RESPONDS TO SUBTLE PRESSURE

WORKS WITH CONSISTENCY

USES LEFT BRAIN MORE THAN RIGHT

RELAXED IN ALL GROUNDWORK

First two levels are universal and apply to every horse and discipline

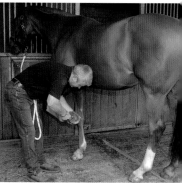

The Pyramid Plan

Why do I need a plan?

The pyramid plan first came to my mind when I was working with problem horses, the ones that dump their riders regularly and dangerously by way of a pastime. It was easy to focus on the main problem, such as the bucking or rearing, and try to tackle it directly without analysing anything else. After all, the eye is always drawn upwards to the top of the pyramid, rather than down to the base right under your nose. However, the key issue might appear at the top of the pyramid, but just below that would be other evasions that were overlooked as they seemed insignificant in comparison to the main problem. Actually, they had a huge part to play. I soon learned that it is cracks in the foundations that cause the instability further up, and it is pointless to tackle the problem without sorting the cause.

So what exactly do you mean by building firm foundations, and how do I do it?

Well read on, as this entire book is devoted to just that! But to get you thinking along the right lines, a firm foundation to your training pyramid comes from such things as having total respect from your horse on the ground and complete control over his movement and direction. Any cracks in the foundations can be strengthened or even rebuilt – you've guessed it – from the ground using halter training and long-lining.

Once the base of the pyramid is strong, I move to the next level, and incorporate the ground training into the ridden work. By the time you've worked back up to the final level of training and often long before, the horse's main problem (such as rearing for example), has usually disappeared. This is what makes this process more progressive and a lot safer than the conventional approach of plucking up the courage to get on, stick it out and hope for the best.

Can you give me an example?

Let's say a horse has been sent to me with a rearing habit. Invariably, the owner calls each week to ask if the horse has reared yet, and apart from the odd occasions the answer is generally 'No'. This is because I take the owner's word for the fact that the horse rears. I don't need to make him rear to solve the problem. As long as I take the time to work through the processes outlined in this book, rebuilding the foundations into something broad and strong, I get long-lasting results that the owner can build upon, regardless of the discipline or level they are riding at.

TIPS FOR PYRAMID PLANNING

1. Have realistic expectations

However big your dreams, every plan needs to be realistic. After all, most of us have to work with constraints such as lack of time, money or facilities, so when drawing up your plan of action you

need to make allowances for this. Real life has a habit of getting in the way, so focus on what you have managed to do in spite of these constraints, rather than being upset about what you haven't yet managed to achieve. Be prepared to be flexible, too.

2. Allow a generous time budget

When you are learning or teaching something new, it takes time, and you have to build that into your plan. Teaching your horse to have perfect manners isn't going to happen in one or two sessions, although you may be pleasantly surprised at how quickly you do start to see a difference. Just like humans, some horses can take in

and process information really quickly, and with others it seems to take ages for the penny to drop. If you stick with it, you will get there in the end, it just may take a little longer.

3. Take small mouthfuls, one bite at a time

Horses are not so different to us when it comes to lessons: they can get bored quite quickly, so keep your sessions short in the beginning. Aim for roughly 15 to 20 minutes, two or three times a week, and for the rest of the week hack or turn out as normal. Don't expect too much from each session, either. Work on one thing at a time and build on it as you start to see progress. When a lesson is over, your horse will go away and think about what has happened, so make sure you have given him a positive experience. Stay focused on your aim, and always end on a good note.

MAXIMIZE YOUR HORSEMANSHIP

In praise of planning

It has only been in the last couple of years that I have truly learned the value of planning. Even when I was in the army, I had a very haphazard approach to organizing my life. As I got older, and work and family made more demands on my time, it became clear that this approach was less than ideal. Work was fine, thanks to our office manager Nikki being highly organized on my behalf. At the beginning of each week she would give me a folder with all the client information I needed, so that part of my life was easy. Meanwhile my wife Sam organized home and family life, so I didn't have to worry about that either. However, it was my personal goals that were falling by the wayside, and I was disappointed at how little I was achieving with my own horses.

Then one summer we went on a family holiday with some of Sam's relatives. Sam's aunt is the headteacher of a primary school, and has only a few years left before retirement. When I asked her what she was going to do with herself, she replied that this was the first time in her life that she hadn't had a five-year plan to guide her. It turned out she always wrote down a plan, starting at the end of the five years and stating where she wanted to be in life at that point, and then worked backwards. Her last five-year plan had been to get a headship so she planned her previous years in terms of the jobs she needed to have done and any exams she needed to obtain to enable her to reach her goal. Each phase of her plan had a time limit and stated the sub-goals that needed to be achieved.

I was really impressed, especially when she explained that she had done that her whole life, and had pretty much achieved everything she set out to do! Sometimes the plan ended up being either shorter or longer than she anticipated, but having a starting point and target to achieve meant she always got there in the end. This brings to mind an important point: however good your plan, it must be flexible, but it's still worth making the plan, even if it needs adapting to fit your personal circumstances at a later stage.

Building your
personal pyramid

The top of the pyramid is the final goal that is specific to your own requirements, while the supporting base is the foundation training that is universal to all horses.

Whether you are aiming to hack safely down the road or take your horse to the top of a competitive career, this is where the basis for respect and obedience must be laid down.

It is only the top level of the pyramid that will change according to your aims and goals, whether they are to sort out a problem or to improve some part of your ridden work. In other words, everyone needs to start at the bottom! From there, you can build your own pyramid and make it the plan for your future training programme.

The way I have designed the pyramid means that if you hit a stumbling block, you'll be able to go back to the previous level and pick something that your horse is good at. Once discipline and confidence are restored, you can work your way back up. Having so many training areas to choose from allows you to be very specific, and enables you to vary the work you do, because although regular and consistent work is important it can also be monotonous.

The best way of motivating both horse and trainer is through small pieces of work. This gives your horse the best chance of being able to work out what is required and achieve something praiseworthy in every session. Try to think of each level of the pyramid as a jigsaw puzzle, with every piece crucial to the bigger picture. If just one piece is missing, the whole thing is incomplete.

A system to suit every type of horse

If you use the pyramid principle, you will always have a versatile and effective training formula to apply, whatever problem or circumstance you are faced with. From simply training a horse to be polite, relaxed, fun and safe to be around, to achieving high competitive performance, the pyramid only needs minor adjustments to suit all the disciplines and the personal needs of the horse.

The main factor that should be taken into account when using this system is the type of horse you have. Understanding his personality is very important, because it bears a direct relation to the type and amount of pressure you need to apply to get him to understand and respond to what you are asking. Some horses are over-reactive, some are under-reactive; some take the principles on board very quickly, others take a while to learn. Knowing these aspects of your horse's personality is the first major step in becoming an effective trainer. How do you find out? Using the pyramid of course!

Taking your horse through the checklist of demands that make up the base of the pyramid and watching his reactions (or inactions) will reveal certain character traits (see page 40). It will also show up problems that are harder to see in other situations, such as when riding. These are the 'holes' in your training that you weren't even aware of. Please do not take this personally: most people have some training 'holes' that need fixing! Just be aware that you may see certain behaviour patterns and attitudes that you haven't seen before, and be thankful that you are in a position to observe them safely and do something about them. The behaviour has probably always been there under the surface, and would come out later when the horse was under pressure. Equally the horse may be coasting along, not doing anything wrong but not doing it particularly well either, and it is these horses that are often the most disgruntled at being found out.

Assessing your horse

When I go out to a client I generally won't have met their horse before, so I have to quickly assess their behaviour and general attitude towards submission. This will also tell me a lot about the horse's character. I always use a training halter to do this assessment, because it allows me to get quicker results, but you can try it with a horseman's halter or a headcollar. Don't be surprised if you get a reaction you weren't expecting.

THE FOUR Rs

Later (page 58), you will read about the four Rs: Request, Response, Release, Reward.

In this case, the Request is pressure on, the Response is moving away, the Release comes when you stop spinning the rope, and the horse is Rewarded by being allowed to stand without any pressure.

The first thing I ask the horse to do is back up in hand with a training halter and a 4m (12ft) lead rope. It is a big thing for a horse to back up, so if you haven't got their full respect, this is where it will show up. Their response to this request will give me a good assessment of their submission and understanding of pressure. If they are reluctant to move backwards and it takes a lot of pressure to get a little response, then I know that the owner/rider is up against it and is having to do a lot of work to get very little back.

To get your horse to back up, look at him and imagine what I call a driving line, just behind his shoulders (see also page 80). On the nearside, step away from the horse's head, towards his quarters with the loose end of the rope in your right hand. As you approach the driving line, start to spin the end of the rope towards the horse's hip (I like the rope to have a tassel on it, see page 81; don't worry if yours doesn't have one, but make sure it is 4m/12ft long). Don't get carried away – large, slow loops using an over-arm action will suffice. When you are doing this there should be no slack rope between your left hand and the horse's nose.

By moving like this you will have created a bend in the horse, which he will naturally want to straighten by swinging his quarters away. Because you have control of the horse's nose in one hand and are pushing his quarters away with the other, he has to move his near hindleg away from the pressure of the spinning rope, and he should do this by stepping under. As soon as the horse has moved, you must stop spinning the rope. Let him stand for as many seconds as it takes for him to absorb the benefit of his actions.

Remember to repeat on both reins.

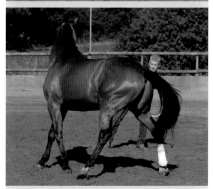

REACTIONS TO EARLY HALTER WORK

Reactions to halter work, such as backing up, vary according to the horse, but include the following:

1. Horse picks it up really quickly

What to do: Reward, and practise asking with greater subtlety.

2. Horse takes his time and moves over sluggishly, not stepping under

What to do: Without pulling, put more of a bend in his neck maintaining the same level of pressure with the rope. By doing this, he will have to step under. Each time he gets it right go back to the first level of bend and try again. If he again moves poorly then increase the bend again. It shouldn't take long for him to work it out. Remember to always remain calm and give the horse his thinking time after each attempt.

3. Horse jumps away and over-reacts

What to do: The temptation is to think you've frightened the horse, but the chances are he has just over-reacted to something new instead of responding. Assess how you asked with the spinning rope, and next time try with less drive and spin. If the horse is still totally over-reactive then just use your hand with open fingers. You will at some point have to address this over-reaction.

4. Horse uses passive resistance, switching off and refusing to move

What to do: No matter what your horse does, it is your job to be consistent and assertive without being aggressive. Passive resistance is off-putting because the horse doesn't make a fuss or jump about, he simply becomes a dead weight. **Remember:** 'Say what you mean and mean what you say' (page 29). If you are getting this passive resistance when working in hand, it will definitely crop up in your ridden work, so now is the time to deal with it.

Make sure you are not in a rush to go anywhere because once you have started you can't give up. First, create more bend and increase the pressure of the spinning rope. If you still don't get a reaction, allow the tassel to touch the horse, not as if hitting him, but annoying him with the flick of the tassle until he moves his quarters away. As soon as he moves those quarters away, immediately stop the rope spinning and give him his thinking time. Don't be tempted to get straight back on his case.

Once you have your horse responding quickly and efficiently, do exactly the same on the other side.

You will be able to gauge your progress by how easy backing up becomes. In the end, it should take a fraction of the pressure you first used. Remember, too, that it is quality of work you are looking for: your horse should back up in a straight line with his head in a sensible position, but this is what you are aiming for – it won't happen straightaway. Eventually, you'll be able to walk towards your horse and ask him to back up just using your body language.

This process suits all horses, regardless of age (from top to bottom): reactive, under-reactive, over-reactive, or stiff and un-supple

Chapter 2

THE TRAINING MINDSET

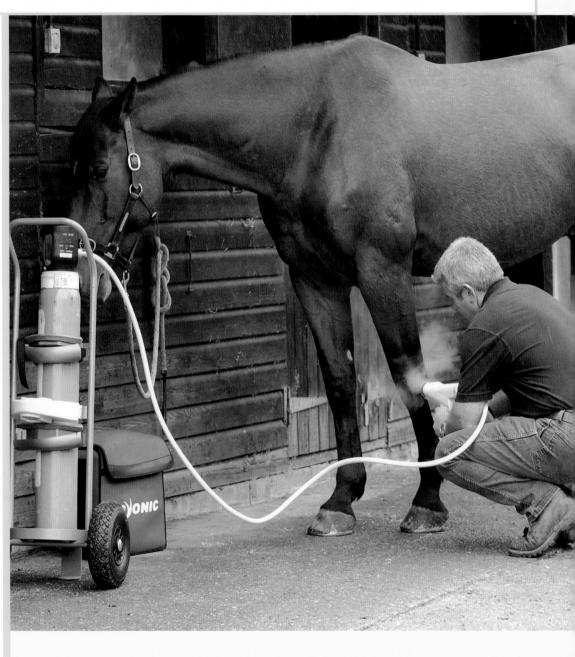

Anybody can own a horse, and most people can learn to ride given a bit of time, yet too few people seem to have an interest in training one. In my opinion, we all owe it to our horses to educate ourselves enough to be able to produce a well-mannered, safe horse that is a pleasure for anyone to handle, ride or own. It's our responsibility to meet this minimum requirement, if only to help the horse understand what is expected of him and avoid any confusion and distress which may otherwise blight his working life and potentially lead to abuse.

You don't have to have the next Olympic hopeful in your stable to aspire to further knowledge, or to become someone who can deal with a wide variety of horses and schooling problems, or to learn how to teach a horse to calmly accept treatments if necessary. One of the main aims of this book is to give you the skills you need to be an effective trainer of horses, not just a rider. I want to encourage riders away from the habit of just going through the motions of riding and owning a horse, and to have more direction and purpose in their approach. Here are some basic rules to form the core of your training handbook.

Educate yourself...
before your horse

For many riders, simply enjoying a safe hack is their final goal, and one that takes a surprising amount of hard work to achieve.

The certainty of enjoying a nice hack is born through plenty of work from the ground

The majority of my clients are not competition riders; they are people who work hard to keep a leisure horse, but are not enjoying him as much as they had hoped. This happens for a number of reasons, the most common of which is that many owners do not realize that having a nice hack comes from putting in lots of work in other areas. Inexperience causes them to miss many of the warning signs along the way, until they end up with a problem that has damaged their confidence, and requires professional intervention.

When horse behaviour does not go according to human plan, it is the responsibility of the human and not the horse to adjust the training methods. Inadequately educated owners often do not know how to deal effectively with the unexpected, and this is what leads to trouble. Another common problem is that as the rider gains confidence, they would like to do more with the horse, but don't have the skills to make that transition. It takes more than just hacking out and going round in circles in the school. You can have a well-mannered horse that does a bit of everything, but only if you are prepared to become your horse's trainer and not just his rider.

Even if you have got the next Olympic hopeful in your stable, the rules are universal and still apply. It's actually a very simple process of deciding what you would like to achieve, sticking to some basic ground rules and dipping into your pool of skills and suggestions. Developing your skills so that you have an adequate supply to get your horse to the level you want is entirely your responsibility. Once you have a realistic idea of what you want to achieve, it's down to you (with the help of an insightful instructor who truly understands your goals) to assess yourself honestly.

How many of the required skills do you already possess, and how much will you need to acquire through additional coaching? Most importantly, are you prepared to develop the self-discipline required to apply the methods outlined in this book with confidence, competence, consistency, commonsense and a thorough understanding of what you are trying to achieve? In my experience most 'problem' horses are not born but created by people who fail to understand the importance of their own behaviour.

The relationship between you and your horse is supposed to be fun and enjoyable.

Remember that your horse is learning every time you are with him; being a good trainer is all about **quality, not quantity**

Ask questions,
expect answers

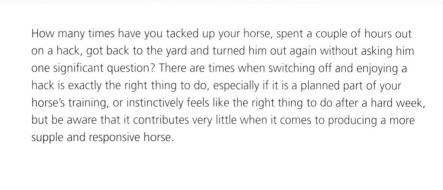

If you don't know where you are trying to get to, how will you know how far you have come or, indeed, when you have arrived?

How many times have you tacked up your horse, spent a couple of hours out on a hack, got back to the yard and turned him out again without asking him one significant question? There are times when switching off and enjoying a hack is exactly the right thing to do, especially if it is a planned part of your horse's training, or instinctively feels like the right thing to do after a hard week, but be aware that it contributes very little when it comes to producing a more supple and responsive horse.

Most leisure horses have more than enough time to themselves each day; for the short time when you are with your horse, it's not much to ask him to listen and learn. You're not being hard on him, unless what you are asking is unfair for his stage of fitness or level of understanding. In fact, I believe that horses like to be mentally stimulated and it is when boredom sets in that horses can misbehave and become unruly and rude.

Set non-negotiable ground rules

Trying to be your horse's best mate may make you feel better, but will it do the same for him?

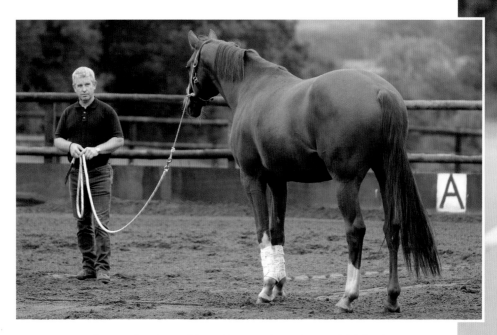

Horse owners often confuse love with sentiment; ask any horse which he'd rather have, an owner he can trust and respect, or one who breathes gently up his nose each morning and always buys him this season's top turnout rug?

I'm not saying you cannot be affectionate to your horse. I love spending time with Jo in the stable, grooming and massaging – but I enjoy it more because we trust and respect each other. To become a successful trainer, you need to establish trust and respect, and this is all about setting ground rules and consistently sticking to them. Of course, a good relationship with your horse is paramount, but once you have established respect you will find that this happens quite naturally. You will also discover that like any truly successful relationship, it will have become a two-way thing instead of you doing all the giving.

Get serious

We've discussed the principles of training and the importance of planning, how to create and use a training pyramid to direct your horse's schooling, and how your own strengths and weaknesses affect the horse.

Now if you think I'm getting too focused on performance rather than fun and am trying to push you into getting competitive, I'm not. If all you want to do is go for a hack that's fine; as I've already said, far too few horses are safe, enjoyable hacks so in my opinion this is a very respectable target. All I'm trying to do is get you to see that you'll have much more fun with a well-trained horse, and you'll be far safer doing it.

If all this talk about becoming your horse's trainer sounds like hard work, remember that in the long term you are making life infinitely easier and more pleasant not only for yourself, but for your horse. You owe him this. A rude horse is open to abuse. If you own a horse that vets and farriers dread to come out to, you are the only person to blame. Even if you bought him with this behaviour, it is still up to you to re-train your horse so that he is a pleasure to be around.

If competition success is your aim, then yes, that will come too as a natural by-product of having a well-trained horse – but the majority of my clients are not competition riders at all. They are people who have realized that to develop their horse into a riding club stalwart who 'does a bit of everything' in a safe manner, they must be prepared to be his trainer and not just his rider.

Discover the inner child

Like children, horses like to be mentally stimulated and are good learners if they get a good teacher.

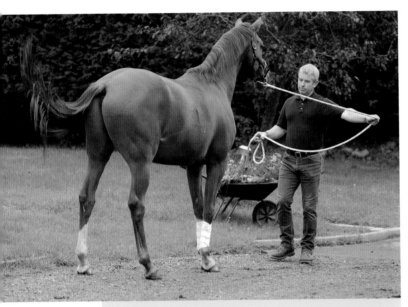

I don't expect respect only when I am training, but in every aspect of being around my horse.

It is when boredom sets in that horses can misbehave and become unruly and rude, again like children. There are a lot of television programmes these days about how to deal with badly behaved children. You know the ones, where a child psychologist is brought in to help the situation as the toddler kicks and screams on the floor and the exhausted mother bursts into tears in the corner. As you watch, it becomes clear that the most common problem with these children is that they live in a house with no rules, no discipline and a lot of shouting. Let's face it, that does sound like some livery yards!

You might think that kids would love a lawless régime, but when the psychologist comes in and sets strict rules and boundaries, the kids thrive on it. The improvement in their behaviour is often phenomenal, and almost immediate.

When the parents take over, things quite often go wrong again for a while. This is because, in reality, it's the parents who need to change their behaviour to enable the process to be successful.

It's not just your horse who has some bad habits to break and a lot of learning to do. To be a good trainer you need to become more self-analytical, especially when you are around your horse. By analytical I do not mean critical. Take notice of the reactions you get when you do certain things, and think about how you might do things differently to get a better reaction. As well as the horse, you need thinking time too.

Remember, you won't get anywhere by chucking your equipment back in the tackroom declaring to everyone how useless it all is, and going home in a huff. This is what my five-year-old son sometimes does. Last time it was a pair of roller blades that came hurtling past us as he stormed through the house shouting he was hopeless, the roller blades were rubbish and we were all stupid. I took him back outside, got him in his boots and after five minutes of clear instruction he was whizzing down the hill. Maybe not in perfect style, but he was succeeding in his task.

There are parallels for horse owners. There will be times when it all seems to be going wrong for exactly the same reasons, but stick with it and you will see changes. Going back to the television programmes for a minute: the biggest factor in changing the children's behaviour is not the fact that they like the child psychologist more than they like their parents; in fact it's probably safe to assume that they love their parents far more than this stranger who has come into their lives to instil discipline. What causes the improvement in behaviour is that they respect the psychologist more than they respect their parents. In the same way, imagining you are your horse's best mate is very nice for you, but quite often familiarity breeds contempt and ultimately your horse will take advantage of that. Just because you love your horse and do everything for him does not mean he will show gratitude or automatically respect you, and to become a successful trainer/teacher you first need to establish that trust and respect. Again, this is easiest to achieve from the ground.

If you are trying to teach him something and the horse is not getting it, stop and analyse why. Go back over the ten principles of training on pages 14–33 and see what you could change. Were you being too strong in the way you posed the question? Were you being clear enough? Is the horse ready for the stage you are working him towards? Try again using a different approach.

Try going back to doing the exercise without a rider. It may tell you something.

MAXIMIZE YOUR
HORSEMANSHIP
Learning from children

I have three sons aged between five and nine years, which can be quite a handful. I try to raise them with the same principles in mind that I use on my horses. I don't want to be so strict they feel suffocated but I don't want to be a push-over where they have little or no respect for me, my wife and any other adults. They have guidelines and boundaries, and most importantly consistency; I say what I mean and mean what I say.

When we visit friends and family we frequently get comments about how well behaved our boys are, yet they are proper boys too. We get all the rough and tumble and mucking about that you'd expect, but at the same time they are polite and a pleasure to be around. We don't want children who have no character or personality; on the contrary, that is what makes them individuals.

Like all children, our boys do step out of line from time to time, but because we are consistent in our approach to their behaviour, any problems that arise are easily dealt with, and they have found there is no benefit to inappropriate behaviour. On the other hand, we make sure the rewards for good behaviour are huge. Respect is a two-way thing. Reward is about family time – not money or presents.

Understand respect

The phrase 'show him who is boss' has rather negative connotations, but as a trainer, you need to remember that horses do actually like to know who the boss is.

In a herd situation, lives depend on knowing who's in charge, and the boss horse has to have the respect of the entire herd. When he (or she) says run, the herd needs to obey, without questioning their authority, or they risk becoming lunch for some predator.

It's no different when you are out on a hack. If you say you are the boss, it's essential that your horse believes you. When you say that crisp packet in the hedge isn't dangerous, then you must be right. For respect you need trust, and you will gain trust by abiding by the ten principles of training outlined on pages 14–33. This will give you the ability to take control in situations that have the potential to go wrong, which will make you and your horse a much safer combination to be around.

MAXIMIZE YOUR HORSEMANSHIP
The effect of respect

If you think that having a horse who is pleasant to be around and easy for others to handle is nice, but not essential, I'd like to bring home to you the serious safety issues linked to respect. Being stamped on, kicked or trampled may be quite obvious examples of what can happen when it goes wrong; less obvious are things such as what may happen with a traffic-shy horse.

Quite often we get a call in the office from a rider who is having problems with their horse on the road. This is the one problem I do not like to take on. The main reason for this is because I haven't yet come up with a way to tackle the problem safely, and if I felt it had been solved but later somebody had an accident, I would never forgive myself.

When we get these calls we always question the rider further, and ask if they have problems in other areas. Their answer is usually no, but when we run through the checklist on page 54, it becomes clear that most riders have at least two or three of these respect issues lurking. Because these have become part of the daily routine, they almost don't realize it is happening. I've frequently found that what they have isn't a traffic problem at all but a trust and respect issue. Sort that out and you will be amazed at the knock-on effect. It's back to the pyramid.

If you have a problem in your ridden work, loading or even handling, it's back to the pyramid. Remember that the big problem is the final culmination of all those little things that you didn't even realize were a problem, which have been quietly undermining the foundations of your training and making things wobbly on top. Start with the little things and the bigger ones tend to disappear.

Imagine you are out shopping and see a child being rude, ignorant or even aggressive towards their mother. Wouldn't you just be longing for the parent to take some kind of control and do something about it? Failing that, wouldn't you just love to do something about it yourself? Apart from being painful to watch and listen to, rude behaviour can escalate into a dangerous situation, when that child doesn't listen to his mother and walks out on to a busy road for example. That's no different to a horse that won't stand at a busy junction; he doesn't respect his rider enough to listen to them.

RESPECT: HAVE YOU GOT IT?

How many of you think your horse respects you? Do you even understand the meaning of respect in terms of your relationship with your horse? Many well-meaning owners discover they are making excuses for themselves, or for their horses, without even realizing. Here is a respect checklist for you to answer honestly.

1. When you're setting off on a hack, does your horse always walk calmly and willingly out of the yard gates, alone or in company?
   This shows he trusts and therefore respects you. If you're in company, will he go first or last without any fuss? A horse who is challenging the hierarchy (you) may not.

2. Do you have your horse's complete attention when you are working him, whether ridden or from the ground, in the arena or out hacking?
   His attention is a sign of respect and also an indication that your training programme is retaining his interest and enthusiasm.

3. When your horse is frightened does he still listen to you?
   When your horse still listens to you in a scary situation he is showing you ultimate trust.

4. If you want to remove him from the field shortly after turnout-time, can you catch him just as easily as you can at bringing-in time?
   If your horse struggles with changes in routine this shows holes in your relationship.

5. When you enter his box with a feed, does he come forwards to grab a mouthful?
   A respectful horse will stand back while you put it down in his usual feeding place.

6. Can you groom, rug and handle your horse easily even while he is distracted such as at a show, while eating, or when other horses are coming and going from the yard?
   Your horse should always be aware of where you are whenever you are around, no matter where he is or what else is going on.

7. Can everyone else in the yard handle your horse easily, when you go away on holiday for example? Do they have more trouble than you with certain things? Or less?
   A truly respectful horse knows his place no matter who is in charge that day.

8. Has he ever barged, squashed or knocked you over? (Even if he was startled and you thought it was 'not his fault'?)
   If so, it suggests that he is not as aware or respectful of your space as he should be. He'd never do that to a dominant horse in a herd situation and get away with it.

9. Does he load into a lorry or trailer 100 per cent of the time in an ordinary headcollar, immediately and obediently? Or do you just know you can 'get him in eventually'?
   Consistent behaviour shows that your horse accepts what you ask of him and always shows respect, not just when it suits him.

10. When clipping, grooming or handling him, are there any 'no go' areas where he will make faces and warn you off if you try to touch them, or try to move away from you? What do you do in response?
    If you allow him to move away or if you move away yourself, then your horse is training you, not the other way round!

Avoid the love–respect conflict

Too often I am at a yard where I have been asked to sort out a horse's problem behaviour, and find that when the horse carries out even a mild form of the behaviour, the owner either appears not to notice or says something like, 'But I love him, he's my baby!' (I once saw a horse trailer going down the road with a 'Babies on board' sticker on the ramp!) Unfortunately, when the day comes that their 'baby' really lets them know he has control by not loading or hacking out, or even becoming aggressive towards them, they take it personally. After all, the only thing you've done wrong is love him, isn't it?

Horses don't understand or appreciate love in the sentimental sense, but like children they do understand and appreciate clear boundaries. It's up to you to sell it to them in a way they understand. Remember that to have respect you need trust, and vice versa.

Sophie Alison and Con

Sophie:

I bought 'Our Memoirs' (Con) as a weedy three-year-old. He was an ex-racehorse and I liked the fact that he moved very well and also had a cheeky character. The first thing I did was to give him three months out in the field, and when I brought him back into work, he appeared very well behaved. It didn't take long for him to start getting cocky, however.

Although gelded at two years of age, he had always been quite coltish as a youngster, and the more work I did with him the naughtier he became. At his first ever show he behaved surprisingly well, but his second outing was more challenging, as he started rearing and napping. He didn't behave this way in the ring, only in the warm-up.

I have owned horses all my life and most of them have been Thoroughbreds, so I am confident in dealing with this type of horse. Con never won an argument, but he often tried. He appeared to relish being told off! He also began to rear at home. It seemed there were no compromises – his behaviour was either very good or very bad, never somewhere in the middle.

He evented as a five-year-old, always performing a good dressage and fantastic cross-country, but show jumping proved to be his weakest phase. This was primarily due to the fact that he was backward-thinking and did not move forwards enough, thus finding it difficult to jump with a powerful back end. He was also plagued by injury, and it was when he was coming back into work as an eight-year old after one such injury that his behaviour was increasingly rebellious.

We were all tired of his constant napping. There were days when he wouldn't even want to leave the yard; he would nap in different places out hacking for no apparent reason, and was happy to take me into ditches, trees, bushes and even a nearby river! He would never win his arguments but it was getting tiresome. Then one day I was riding Con and leading another horse and the next thing I knew, Con had launched towards the other horse and mounted him, which he seemed to find hilarious. On another occasion, he launched himself and mounted another

horse in the warm-up of an event. Then he started trying to mount people walking across his paddock.

Another oddity in his behaviour was that he used to do his own interval training when turned out. He would set off for no apparent reason and gallop flat out around the field, stop, change the rein and proceed to do the same again. I am sure he used to time himself! It was funny to watch apart from the fact that I was sure he was going to injure himself. He would also stand in the corner of the field and start pawing the ground at the same time squealing very loudly. His behaviour in the stable was not much better. If he was in his stable while being mucked out, even if tied up, he would try and molest you.

I had had enough and so I called Max.

Max:

Con had complete control over every situation. His behaviour in the field shows he felt completely superior and he truly believed he was in charge. Although Sophie believes she never lost an argument, in Con's eyes he was victorious because he was only at level one of his evasions, whereas Sophie had given it all she had.

Sophie:

During Max's visit, three other people in the yard came to watch 'Cocky Con', and for the first 45 minutes he put up quite a fight. But, suddenly, his eyes changed, it was very strange to watch. Cocky Con suddenly looked at Richard as if to say, what do you want me to do now? After this, he just did as he was told.

Max:

My initial assessment was that Con had absolutely no respect for anyone, man nor beast. Respect had to be the first issue I tackled, so halter work was the first thing I put into place. Con's reaction to that was one of frustration at not being able to use established evasions to control me or the situation. Con, like many horses I see, had only ever had to use phase one of the evasions. The great thing about halter work is that you can still take control, even if the horse chooses to raise his game and go up a level. Once Con realized that his behaviour was not going to change the situation, no matter how hard he tried, he became more compliant and respectful.

Sophie:

What I was impressed with most was how forward Con was moving. Normally when in the school, he is always thinking backwards and certainly does not move forwards unless asked. Max then rode him, having performed his 'rope tricks' and long-reining techniques. Con looked very loose and free moving. I was then told to get on him myself. I was amazed! Con had not been schooled for over a year but he felt fantastic.

Max:

Although Sophie viewed the halter work as 'rope tricks', it certainly is not about tricking the horse or anything magical. It is about putting in place an established pattern of control over direction, both physically and emotionally. It becomes a kind of comfort blanket for the horse as he begins to know the rules and boundaries. It is back to the naughty child who is relieved at boundaries being put into place, and knowing what the rules are.

Con became more forward because his emotional handbrake was now off, which allowed him to be more forward both emotionally and physically. This was mainly due to the circling work we went through, which cancelled out Con's belief in his size, strength and speed. He was also more forward as he was not keeping anything in reserve.

Sophie:

I worked with the rope and long lines every day for a week before I rode Con. I was quite anxious and on our first day out hacking, Con was really put to the test as a car had been dumped in the middle of the river where I cross it. Normally, this would be the perfect opportunity for Con to start napping, but he was perfectly behaved. Six months on, he has not napped once, and as a consequence of us both being able to concentrate instead of arguing, his flatwork is improving.

Max:

The improvement in Con's behaviour started in that first session of halter training, because his normal antics didn't work no matter how hard he tried to push the situation. A horse like Con, who has given it his best shot to win but fails, will have a huge attitude change and as long as Sophie is consistent and fair, this attitude will be for the long term.

Sophie:

The next real test was to take Con out to a competition. I took him show jumping. He had not left home for 18 months and normally behaved like a raving lunatic at a show. Before I mounted, I warmed him up with the rope work, and he behaved impeccably. He also jumped superbly, so not only had his behaviour improved but also his jumping technique. I was very impressed!

Max:

It is so important that horses learn that being away from home is no excuse for bad behaviour. So many people get embarrassed at the thought of doing something different at a show, such as schooling with the rope to remind Con who was calling the shots, but it is essential to avoid a downward spiral, first at the show then gradually at home, too. This little bit of work before doing a dressage test or jumping is a win-win situation for the rider and the horse. It gets the horse focused on what is being asked, warms him up nicely, both physically and mentally, and nips any thoughts of bad behaviour in the bud without arguments. The result is a far more harmonious horse and rider combination for the judges to witness.

Time spent warming up at a show will also be reduced, because the time is being spent constructively and you are not having to battle it out trying to overcome any behaviour issues. Ground training creates an endorphic release that helps calmness and the ability to process information, allowing the rider to control the adrenalin flow that will naturally kick in at a competition.

The principles of communication

Remember the four Rs

Request
  Response
    Release
      Reward

This is the quickest way for me to convey what pressure and release is all about. Everything revolves around this principle, no matter what level you are at or which discipline you have chosen. It runs through all equestrianism the world over.

The order and timing of the four Rs is important. One must follow the other in immediate succession. If you concentrate on doing this you will invariably be fair and consistent in all your dealings with your horse.

In the long term it will also improve your riding, as you will become very subtle and sympathetic with your aids, and your horse will respond readily and gratefully.

Now you've got a good idea of the qualities you need to develop in order to become a good trainer, and the central role that respect will play in your success, we should talk about how to achieve that respect. You acknowledge your horse's behaviour is not entirely as you would like, but what is the best way to put it right?

Rather than talking about correction, it's probably more accurate to discuss communication. I use a system of applying pressure, say from a halter during groundwork or my hand, leg and seat aids when riding. Asking a horse to move away from the leg, give and take with the reins, and half-halt are all forms of pressure and release.

By pressure, I do not mean pain. Pain is counterproductive as it creates fear, damages trust and will not help the horse to learn anything. It is the release of pressure that rewards the horse for correct behaviour.

I have found this system makes most sense to the horse, since it is their language and it is how they communicate and discipline each other within their own environment. It is the essence of all interaction

> Pressure does not mean pain. *Pain is counterproductive as it creates fear, damages trust and will not help the horse to learn anything.*

between horses, and has become the essence of communication between horse and human in my training programme too.

A horse will use mainly two types of pressure when communicating: visual pressure such as face-pulling, putting the ears back and walking into another horse's space to move them around. This is the first action they will take when trying to assert authority. Secondly there is tactile pressure, such as biting and kicking, which they only use to back up the visual pressure.

Horses are very good at putting the pressure on to make their point, then taking it off when they get their result. For example, if a horse further down the pecking order gets into the space of the boss horse in a field, the boss horse will pull a face and will then stop and allow the minion to either take heed or not. If he doesn't heed the warning then the boss will do it again but he might add a bite, normally to the neck. Horses do not keep the pressure on because this doesn't allow the other horse the opportunity to do the right thing and go away. A classic example of being firm but fair, saying what you mean and meaning what you say! A really good time to watch this behaviour being demonstrated is with a group of horses in a field when food is put down. There is always one horse that ignores the faces the boss is making, and continues doing what they are doing until the boss really shows them with a bite or a kick that it isn't a bluff.

There has been much debate over the use of pressure and release in recent years. Some sections of the equestrian community feel that it is a form of negative reinforcement, but for me, negative reinforcement is when the trainer imposes a double negative on the horse and there is never any reward – a 'heads I win, tails you lose' scenario. With pressure and release, the reward is the release. Horses soon get to the point where they begin to anticipate the pressure, and you need to apply so little it can barely be seen. I like to stay open-minded about things, but so far I haven't found any other technique that is quite so complete or effective.

MAXIMIZE YOUR HORSEMANSHIP

Carrot or stick?

I remember a television documentary called 'The Carrot or the Stick?' which made quite an impression on me. Two teams had to face a set of challenges on the moors with really harsh weather conditions. One group was the Carrot Team where there was no negativity allowed, and no consequences if they lost a challenge. They had good sleeping quarters, great food and plenty of hot water, regardless of the outcome of their work. Meanwhile, the Stick Team were worked hard from dawn to dusk. The food was dire, sleeping arrangements were damp and cold, and no matter how hard they worked there was no reward for effort.

The aim of the mission was to see which team would achieve the task the best and ultimately the Sticks won, even though they were literally on their knees by the end. As a team they pulled together and just got on with it, united in adversity, while the Carrots fell apart because there were no consequences to their actions, therefore no incentive to do well.

Both team instructors admitted that they hated training by one method only; the 'stick' instructor explained that he felt bad because he was unable to reward his men for excellent work, while the 'carrot' instructor hated the fact that there were no consequences for poor performance. Both recommended a mixture of both the carrot and the stick as the most effective way of training, and my military experience really backs this up. Everybody needs goals, but at the same time everyone needs reward and praise. There also have to be consequences for bad decisions. I find this combination delivers great results when it comes to training horses.

Learn to let go

Learn the four Rs by heart (see page 58) so that when you are working your horse, it becomes an automatic chain of responses, and a constant dialogue back and forth between you and your horse.

For example:

you **REQUEST** the horse to walk on by touching him with your leg;

your horse **RESPONDS** by moving forwards, so

you **RELEASE** the pressure with your legs

and **REWARD** the horse.

You don't need to use your legs again until your horse either slows down (when you Repeat Request) or you Request something different, then the whole dialogue starts again.

With time and practise, the sequence will become seamless and so ingrained that you won't even realize you are applying it. You and your horse will be in a bubble of perfect communication and co-operation which is what we are all aiming for, after all.

As trainers and riders, we can be too busy giving commands (ie applying the pressure) to remember that the momentary release of the pressure is as important as the pressure itself, as this is the moment that teaches the horse and directs his behaviour.

There is nothing worse than seeing a rider nag a horse with their legs every step of the way or fiddle with their hands non-stop. That is pressure with NO release, and eventually your horse will switch off. With the help of the tips in this book you will learn to apply the minimum of pressure to get a response, and perfect your timing so that your horse gets an immediate release as he moves off. Unless you need a change in pace or direction, you shouldn't need to keep re-applying the leg.

A common mistake when trying to teach a horse something new is to start too close to the end goal. For example, if you wanted to teach a horse to jump a five-foot fence, you wouldn't start by riding him into a five-foot fence after no preparation then wonder why he refused or knocked it down! Yet so many people make an equivalent mistake when training horses in other skills. It is not what you can make your horse do which counts, but what your horse will do happily, willingly and consistently well.

At one demonstration I worked with a young pony that had been very difficult to lead in hand. At the end, a woman asked me about training foals and weanlings to lead, as she bred youngsters and liked to show them in hand, but always had a problem leading them.

I started to explain how I would start out with a long rope attached to a headcollar and walk out ten feet in front of them until they learned to follow me. This might take two or three days, then I would repeat it making the rope shorter. At this point, the lady interrupted me and said, 'That's all very well, but I have to lead my horses at the shoulder.' She then went on to describe how she would hold on to their head with one hand and drive them forwards with a schooling whip in the other hand, but she could not work out why this didn't work. When she had said all this I carried on with my explanation, saying that I would shorten the rope every two or three days until the youngster was walking at my shoulder of his own free will. It may have taken a couple of weeks to achieve, but it was a good habit that would last a lifetime.

Comfort the horse's mind, body and soul

It is well worth doing some suppling exercises to loosen up your horse before you begin work. These stretches encourage the horse to extend his spine, and articulate the poll, as well as loosening the shoulders, elbows and neck. This neck muscle (below) should be soft and floppy. If it is tight your horse will be tight elsewhere.

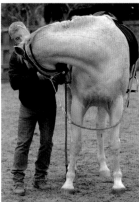

In an ideal world we would all be able to keep our horses in a field with suitable shelter and plenty of equine mates, all day every day.

However, for the vast majority of us this isn't possible or practical. Many livery yards have limited turnout during the winter, and to have our horses turned out all year round can be difficult if you work and time is too short to start catching, cleaning and drying your horse before you tack up each day. However, if you want your horse to cope with the pressures of working for you and living in a stable, you have to take his emotional and physical wellbeing seriously.

I keep both of my horses at livery and they do have to stay in quite a lot over the winter, which is why I have tried to develop a varied training programme to keep them fit and occupied (see Muscle Maintenance, at right). It's important to remember that physical fitness is only half the story; as a good trainer, you must also consider the other half – the emotional side of training. Long term this can do the most damage, as a horse's mind is a fragile thing and once damaged, it is very hard to fix. Lumps, bumps, strains and sprains take a fraction of the time in comparison.

I feel that the most useful thing I can do with my own horses to make sure that they are physically, mentally and emotionally sound is to work them correctly so that I put less strain on them through bad posture. I also have them checked out regularly by an equine dentist and chiropractor.

Talking about correct posture may sound stuffy, but I see so many horses whose problems stem from being ridden/ worked incorrectly (allowing your horse to have poor posture even out hacking is detrimental to his wellbeing). Each year, I watch hundreds of horses being ridden in a way that I know is going to result in their physical discomfort and injury, and emotional trauma. The owners of these horses are always totally surprised when their much-loved animal develops behavioural problems.

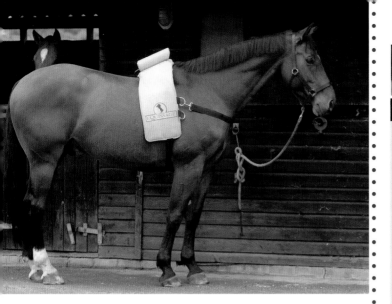

MUSCLE MAINTENANCE

I am not a great gadget man but when I find something that really helps me in my work and keeps my horses happy then I will shout about it. One of the things that I have found that has made a real difference to my horses and their wellbeing in training is the Equissage machine. I am very lucky to have access to one at my livery yard, for a small fee shared with other livery owners.

The Equissage machine works by using vibration to increase blood and lymph circulation. The vibrations travel through the body and gently stimulate blood and lymph flow to take away soreness, and increase healing and repair. It also increases the blood flow for up to an hour after the treatment, which helps remove any build-up of lactic acid – the cause of cramping and soreness after hard work. It is even helpful for those horses that aren't worked through the week and are then worked hard on a weekend, particularly those prone to azoturia, or tying up.

The Equissage machine can be used to warm up a horse before exercise, so I always pop it on for 20 minutes while I am sorting myself out before riding, and by the time I get on to ride, my horses are already warmed up. I find the Equissage allows me to ask more of my horses, for longer, without any detriment to their physical wellbeing.

The end result of massage is that by improving blood flow, stiff joints and sore muscles are alleviated, which will give you a bigger stride pattern from the minute you start to ride, and warm-up time is reduced by about a third.

MAXIMIZE YOUR HORSEMANSHIP

The danger of dehydration

I am definitely a horseman who is constantly learning, and one of the areas that I have really researched recently is the effect of dehydration in horses. It was the husband of a client who made me aware of the number of horses that suffer from dehydration. I have to be honest and say it is not something I have thought about much before, other than making sure my own horses had plenty of fresh clean water available.

The horse, like every other mammal, is an assembly of trillions of individual cells making up the tissues and organs of the body. The health of each cell depends on the correct surrounding fluid being brought to it by the blood circulation. If the surrounding fluid does not consistently bathe all of the cells with the correct mixture of electrolytes, like sodium and potassium, the cells will either absorb too much water and burst, or lose too much water and shrivel and die, which in turn affects adjacent organs and tissues. Between these two lethal extremes, cells can become much less efficient and so affect local and overall performance.

Testing for dehydration with a simple pinch test.

When the workload in horses increases, a cell imbalance in the muscles, which is of no importance at rest, can become acute and severe and may have serious consequences such as tying up. The higher the demands for athletic performance, the greater the need for the correct balance of body fluid composition.

Horses in training are frequently found to have moved away from this balance. If a horse that usually does well seems to be suffering from reduced performance, it is easy to check for dehydration by pinching the skin. If the horse is healthily hydrated, it should instantly snap back into place. If it doesn't, dehydration is indicated. You can buy therapeutic patches (*below*) that use the horse's own cell signalling system to prompt its body to correct the balance of electrolytes. The patch, which sticks to the quarters, doesn't use any drugs. I have found they make a huge difference to my horse's performance. For more information, see www.performancepatches.co.uk

Michael Potter and Vista Grande

Michael:

Vista Grande is an eight-year-old, 16.2hh Belgian Warmblood. This complex but ultimately endearing mare was purchased for me as a five-year-old (very) novice show jumper. Even then, I knew she had a difficult temperament. She was aggressive in the stable and argumentative under saddle.

I spent the first few months schooling her quietly and jumping her over small courses without any major problems. Providing I did not ask too much of her, such as to lengthen or shorten, or for too much collection, she was fine and rarely touched a fence. It was when the courses became bigger and I needed to ask a little more of her that the problems began.

Her main course of evasive action was to rear, so high she had to teeter about on her hind legs to stop herself falling over backwards. This was not too bad at home but in a crowded collecting ring she became a danger to other riders. I sought professional help from a very experienced show jumper, but they were unable to persuade her to behave either. The only invaluable piece of advice they gave me was that as long as I kept her moving forwards she would be unable to rear. This worked really well when space permitted, but you can't always guarantee that in the collecting ring or while waiting to enter the arena. Collecting ring stewards began to take cover as soon as she appeared, or tried to make sure she could be ridden directly into the ring. Competing was starting to become stressful and that did not help the sensitive mare at all. She had had her back and teeth checked when she came in the yard so I had no reason to suspect her problems were caused through discomfort or pain. Rearing was starting to become a habit – it became her first course of action when something unsettled her on a hack.

Max had been on the yard twice before to help with loading problems and although I knew the basics of his training methods, and I had put his teaching to good use with reluctant loaders, I felt out of my depth with Grande.

As usual Max checked for physical problems first and I was horrified that he found Grande's neck and shoulders were very stiff and would have been causing her considerable discomfort and pain over years rather than months. She was not the easiest patient, but Max managed to loosen her off and make her more comfortable. I only wish I could say she was grateful but at least she did not bite him, another of her less than endearing habits.

He also noticed there was a thin line of white hair about six inches long following the line of the headpiece. This led us to think that in all probability someone had used some fairly extreme methods and gadgets to make her behave, hence her general distrust of the human race. I also explained to Max that she was impossible to clip unless sedated by the vet as she became so sweated up, and even when sedated she fought the extra dose needed to allow me to do her head and ears. Even plaiting her was not an option, let alone pulling her mane or trimming her topknot. I was reassured that Max really liked Grande in spite of all her quirks, but even he couldn't come up with any overnight miracles.

Max:

Miracles are few and far between, but huge differences in a horse's way of going can happen after months of dedicated and consistent work.

Michael:

Max went through his usual exercises on the ground to remind her who was in charge and to ensure he had her respect. I know these exercises are integral to me being in charge, but I have to confess I tend only to resort to them when all else fails, instead of using them regularly like I should. Having said that, the halter and rope always come out when a horse will not go on the lorry, and doing the ground exercises pre-loading has not failed me yet!

Max:

The groundwork in the early stages was an absolute necessity to even begin to unravel the emotional mess this mare had become. It was vital to get her to realize

we were not going to punish her for her behaviour, but at the same time we weren't going to let her control the situation. We did this by doing the basic circling work on a halter and 12-foot rope, showing her we could control all directions. We then moved on to long-lining to help her posture and way of going.

I know Michael doesn't like the groundwork and only uses it when necessary, and this is the biggest mistake that a lot of people make. Only using it as a contingency plan when things go wrong means that Michael will always be taking two steps backwards and only one step forwards. Used regularly it will become part of a cure rather than a temporary stop-gap.

Michael:

Max then mounted and Grande proceeded to demonstrate her spectacular rear. He recommended I put her in a Myler combination bit which would give me more control with a very light hand. She responded very well and even managed a little shortening and lengthening, both with Max and myself. The rearing stopped as she realized she was more comfortable both in her body and in her mind. However, there was no miraculous change in Grande's temperament in the ensuing weeks and she continued to rear occasionally, especially if she was frightened. She remained fairly manic in crowded collecting rings but her behaviour at home and in the ring improved.

Max:

I know it is really difficult to do something that will cause people to look and stare at a show, but as our other case histories have shown, it is worth it if you really want to crack the problem. If Michael had done groundwork at the shows he would have seen Grande's behaviour improve in the crowded collecting rings and her jumping become consistently better. I have several clients that now use groundwork to work their horses in at shows and their results have improved, along with their horse's general behaviour.

Michael:

Grande had now started to listen to my aids and I could jump her safely over bigger courses. She was beginning to trust my riding, and with Max a regular visitor on the yard to look after her physical wellbeing and me doing the daily stretching exercises that Max showed me, the clear rounds kept coming. After a couple of months she was respectful enough for me to stop using the combination bit and I put her in a milder snaffle. She continues to be a difficult mare but none of her quirks are a problem to me as long as Max keeps her comfortable. I am sure that her mental problems are only out of habit or of her own making. Max never tried to tell me that she would become gentle and submissive, but with his support I am able to work within the parameters of what she is prepared to do. Her behaviour is so greatly improved and she is so much improved in her general attitude to all that is going on around her, I feel she is easily capable of going on to bigger and better achievements.

Max:

In 2006 Michael has achieved some fabulous results. However, I think they would have come sooner if he had incorporated the ground training into his training programme. That said, well done Michael on your successes!

Chapter 3

BUILDING THE FOUNDATIONS

Hopefully, you are now convinced you want to be more than just a rider, and you have an idea of the concepts and principles that make a good trainer. Now it's time to get down to work and make it happen. In this chapter I explain how to build the first layer of your pyramid, and start work towards your individual aims.

As I explained in chapter 1, the top of the pyramid represents your final goal, while the base of the pyramid is the foundation training that is universal to all horses, whether you are aiming to hack safely down the road or take your horse to the top of a competitive career. This is where the basis for respect and obedience is laid down. The middle of the pyramid directs you towards your specific end goals. The design of the pyramid means that if you hit a stumbling block, you'll be able to go back a stage and regain your horse's confidence.

Level 1:
Creating solid foundations

The most important part of your pyramid is the base. This represents your foundations. If the base is not broad and able to support the level above it, it will collapse when put under pressure, and this is particularly common with novice horse owners. So many of them have dreamed of having a horse for years, but when they finally realize this dream, the reality of horse ownership is a disappointment because the horse starts to misbehave and push the boundaries enough to take the fun out of simple pleasures such as hacking. Keeping the boundaries in place is a case of constantly checking the pyramid foundations. Many owners don't realize that buying a well-schooled horse is not enough – those foundations require life-long maintenance.

For a horse to be a pleasure to handle and safe to ride, he needs to respond to what is being asked of him in any given situation. You would never get into a car with no steering or brakes and take it for a drive, yet riders do the equivalent all the time with their horses. Putting in place the base of your pyramid should be the first and most important thing you do, regardless of your ability or ambitions.

Once your horse is working correctly from the ground and responding to your aids and signals, you will be able to use these skills to improve his abilities and overcome any training difficulties.

BENEFITS OF ESTABLISHING A FIRM TRAINING BASE

1.	Makes every day you spend with your horse a pleasure, maximizes enjoyment and ensures you get value for money out of your hobby
2.	Develops personality, strength of character and confidence in the horse, rather than taking his character away
3.	Horse's respect and willing co-operation extends to everybody that deals with him, so protects him from abuse
4.	Allows for development so that, together, horse and rider can become more ambitious and achieve more if they want to
5.	Keeps horse mentally, emotionally and physically sound enough to enjoy an extended working life

MAXIMIZE YOUR HORSEMANSHIP

Invest in your own pleasure

I can already hear you thinking that your horse is your hobby, so why bother getting serious about schooling? Because horses are an expensive and time-consuming hobby, and to get the maximum amount of pleasure out of them, they need to be consistently well mannered. This is something you really can and should do something about, however much of a novice you are.

I'll tell you a quick story about a friend of mine. All her life she wanted to be around horses, and her biggest ambition was to own a horse of her own. She became a very successful businesswoman and could eventually afford a horse, but as so often happens, she bought one that was beyond her current skill levels. He was an intelligent animal and it didn't take long for him to realize she was a novice, and to completely take control of every situation. Her life's dream was rapidly turning into a nightmare and she just didn't know what to do about it. She felt so out of control and got things so out of perspective that she even started to believe fate had something to do with it; if the traffic lights were green as she drove to the yard it would be a good day, if they were red she began to panic because it was sure to be a bad day, and so on. How much of an enjoyable hobby is that?

Eventually her husband couldn't stand it any longer. He couldn't believe she was getting into such a state about going to see the horse she had waited her whole life to own. He persuaded her to get help with the horse and this enabled her to regain control by rebuilding those foundations that had crumbled. Together they built a good strong relationship of mutual respect, and now she knows she can guarantee a good day with her horse no matter what colour the traffic lights are.

The universal base of the pyramid

So now you're convinced it's the best way forwards, let's get building our way towards a more polite and trustworthy horse. The seven key elements that form the base of the pyramid are as follows, regardless of your discipline:

KEY ELEMENTS

1. You have the ability to move your horse's feet in all directions – forwards, sideways and backwards

2. Your horse responds to minimal pressure by moving away from it in all directions – forwards, sideways and backwards

3. Your horse shows trust and respect towards the handler in all situations and circumstances

4. You and your horse develop greater subtlety so less pressure is required

5. You both work with consistency

6. Your horse learns to adopt a pattern of thinking primarily directed by the logical left-hand side of his brain rather than the instinctive right-hand side

7. Your horse stays relaxed during all aspects of groundwork

1. Move the horse's feet in all directions

This is the cornerstone of all the training and re-training that you and your horse will go through. Horses put a very high value on the being who controls direction and makes the decision about who is going where; make sure that it is you controlling and directing movement, not the horse. Controlling can be done in very subtle but nonetheless significant ways by the horse.

When we think about moving our horse's feet it is not just about halter work or long-lining; it also comes into play doing everyday yard duties. For example, next time you go down to the yard count how many times you walk around your horse if you are picking out his feet or grooming him. I bet the majority of you walk round to the other side while he stands still! So who is moving their feet? You are, so your horse will automatically assume that he is the boss and you are the underdog.

Likewise, when you're clearing up, do you sweep around him or make him move out of your way, so you can sweep the space he was standing on? Yes that's right, he should be moving out of your way, not the other way round! If you insist on this, you will start to be seen through different eyes straightaway. Some horses will question your right to tell them where to move to, and you must accept the challenge and remain firm but fair.

Training: Level 1

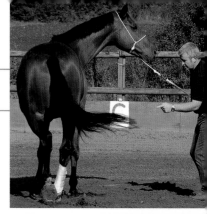

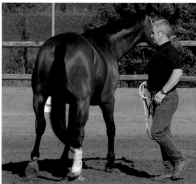

KEY ELEMENT

2. Move away from minimal pressure in all directions

Following on from the previous exercise, the horse must move away from pressure in whatever form it takes. This could be your finger, a click of your voice asking him to move over, the touch of a heel or spur or simply your physical presence moving into his personal space. What you have to teach your horse here is that moving away from the pressure will cause release so that you can reward him by taking the pressure off.

A quick word about spurs and schooling whips: I am not against these providing they are used responsibly to back up or refine your aids, but they should never be used as a form of punishment.

3. Show trust and respect towards the handler in all situations and circumstances

Now there's a surprise – you probably thought this would be first on my list! I confess, in the beginning it was, but I soon realized that to get trust and respect, you had to understand the first two elements. Elements 1 and 2 will assert your position in your relationship with your horse. When you start to move through the levels described in the pyramid, you are going to be asking a lot of your horse, both physically and emotionally, and for him to respond positively to this, you need trust and respect, otherwise you'll get halfway through your training programme and realize you can't progress any further.

Your horse is entitled to question what you are asking, and you are obliged to provide a coherent answer, but neither side is entitled to be rude.

4. Develop greater subtlety so less pressure is required

You can now start to think about making what you are asking of the horse more subtle. You probably won't remember how obvious you were having to be in the early sessions of your training, and how unco-ordinated it all felt. Like anything new, it takes time for it to become second nature. Learning to drive is a classic example. I never thought I was going to be able to do the clutch–gear thing, but these days I am halfway down the road and I don't even remember starting the engine.

Quite often after I have finished working with a client they'll say that I make everything look very obvious, which is true, but I need to do that so the client has an opportunity to take in the information. If I were to work away and just hope they were able to take in everything, or even worse, let them try and guess how I had done it, I would have many unhappy clients.

Once I'm happy with the basics of what they are doing, it's only then that I can start to refine the subtleties of the lessons. Think again of learning to drive. Initially your driving instructor might ask you to look in your mirror, indicate, check the mirror again and take the next left turn. Later on, the instructor might just ask you to turn left and know you have the knowledge to check the mirror and signal before doing so. As your experience grows, he is able to be less obvious about what he wants and you require less explanation. But can you imagine the chaos that would have ensued if on the first lesson he had just told you to take the next left turn, without any instruction? Well, sometimes we can be a bit like that with our horses; we expect them to know it all already.

When training your horse, remember that he is not stupid just because you have to begin by being very obvious. It won't take long before the obvious becomes much more subtle.

You may have to begin by teaching your horse to back up using your whole hand (top), but you will gradually progress to being able to make your request with just your fingertips.

Tracey Richards and Rupert

Tracey:

Rupert is a five-year-old, 17hh Belgian Warmblood, and I fell in love with him as soon as I tried him. However, when I got him home he took an immediate dislike to my other horse. It seemed likely that he had not been socialized properly with other horses and that he had been kept stabled for his entire life.

His way of going felt like he had been ridden in draw reins a lot with a fairly strong bit and he was also a little dead to the leg. I started riding him in a loose ring synthetic snaffle to try and encourage him to accept the bit rather than backing off my contact.

Apart from that, all was going well with his ridden work – he was very well schooled for his age (possibly too well). However, his attitude to other horses was getting worse. The horse next door could not even put his head out of his stable without Rupert kicking out at him with ears flat back. His aggression was also aimed towards me and he would not allow me to touch him in certain areas.

After four months his ridden work was suffering too. He was getting worse and worse at moving forwards off the leg, so on one occasion I tapped him with a whip to back up my leg, and he flipped. He did several 'handstands' in a row, and would not go forwards. I asked a friend to ride him as I thought it could be me. He started napping and threatening to rear, and in the end she dismounted for her own safety.

I knew something must be wrong but I had already had his teeth checked, the saddler assured me his saddle fitting was fine and neither an equine massage therapist nor a qualified physiotherapist could find anything physically wrong with him. I gave him a few days off and tried again. On the way to the field where we ride, Rupert stopped, napped, and threatened to rear. I sat there and waited, as I was unsure what response I would get to my leg aids, and he then walked on. But this behaviour recurred several times before I'd done one lap of the field, so I decided to call it a day and call out Max.

When Max went into the stable with Rupert to assess him, Rupert tried to push Max around, and Max responded with a swift elbow a couple of times before Rupert learnt not to intrude into Max's space. Max said these elements of stallion-like behaviour suggested that Rupert was gelded late, which I have since learnt to be true. He also found that his shoulders and poll were sore, which could be likened to having a constant migraine.

After Max had stretched his forelegs and poll to alleviate this soreness, Rupert was taken into the school in a pressure halter and 12-foot rope. Max spent some time getting him to respond to the pressure halter before putting the saddle on, when Rupert once again put up a fight. Max explained that Rupert associates the saddle with pain in his sore shoulders. Max then moved on to long-lining and eventually to riding Rupert. He walked around on a long rein allowing Rupert to stop and nap to the gate or mares, but then used the wip-wop (see page 96) to drive him forwards, which worked wonders. When I got on board, I could not believe how forward going Rupert was. He had turned from a 'Can't, Shan't, Won't' horse to a 'What next?' horse in a matter of hours!

I did the groundwork religiously for a month, and it really started to pay off. His attitude towards me in-hand was much more respectful and he even improved with other horses. I kept the groundwork going, even when I reintroduced ridden work, doing a little every time to gain authority before getting in the saddle. Now I can just get straight on, but I still keep a varied schooling programme to keep Rupert occupied.

The improvements have been huge. I can now safely ride him on the road, and although he still has his moments, I feel confident enough to deal with his tantrums. He is now forward-going, light and responsive in the school and I can even tie my other horse outside Rupert's stable without a fight. We have also started to jump which he enjoys, so the future looks bright.

KEY ELEMENT

5. Work with consistency

If you work with consistency, so will the horse. If you arrive at the yard and think you can't be bothered, then you will let your horse take charge. You will probably find that by being consciously consistent all of the time, there will be a time when you have done a whole session down the yard and not even thought about it. One day you will be wondering if he is ever going to get it, and then all of a sudden you won't be able to remember the last time you had to ask twice. Everything happened as you wanted it to and you didn't have to explain yourself.

This is a huge and important stepping stone, a bit like a child riding his bike without stabilizers for the first time! They wobble about, fall off and have a temper tantrum, then all of a sudden just get on and off they go. It gives you an immense feeling of achievement.

Once you have reached this important step with your horse, you will be able to progress to the next level of your training. But you can only move ahead in your training once your horse is consistently performing well at the previous level, and has stopped wobbling without his stabilizers.

6. Use left brain more than right brain

the winning post first isn't using the left side of his brain to logically work out how far behind him the next horse is. He is using the right side.

As trainers we need to work on stimulating the left side to develop the horse's thinking and learning ability. For a horse to be obedient, polite and relaxed when being trained or schooled, he needs to use more left-brain thinking, and this is only possible for your horse when he is totally at home with everything you are asking in all aspects of handling and riding, whether it is in the school or out on a hack.

I go into more detail about left- and right-brain thinking on pages 104–107, but to give you a quick insight, when it is working, the left side of the horse's brain has an endorphic effect on him. That is to say it releases endorphins, the body's feel-good chemicals, which allow him to become more comfortable and more efficient at thinking and analysing situations that would otherwise be contrary to his nature (such as loading into a horsebox). This use of the left side of the brain will enable your horse to cope with situations that would normally cause him to react, and it is what he engages when he is being asked to move his feet or move away from pressure.

When he is using the right side of his brain, he is in fight or flight mode, and the adrenalin rush prevents him from thinking or learning very much. So for example, a racehorse straining to pass

Although Jo has been spooked and gone into right-brain mode, he hasn't totally lost focus and I can still work him on the lines in a controllable way, which will help him to calm down and gradually begin to come back into left-brain thinking.

KEY ELEMENT

7. Stay relaxed during all aspects of groundwork

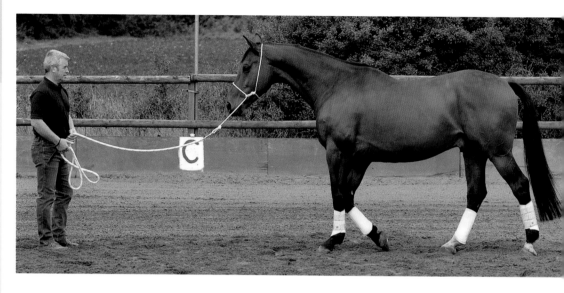

I have just talked about how getting your horse to use left-brain thinking will enable him to relax, and groundwork is how you achieve this. If your horse can't relax in his work it will become a nightmare for him, as horses are not good at handling stress. I often hear about horses not being able to cope with pressure, but it is not so much the pressure that is the problem. It is the stress of being constantly put in the position of using the right side of the brain, where instinctive thought lives and rules. While he is in this state, anything we ask him to do won't make a lot of sense, and confusion is one of the main breakdowns in training.

Introducing ground training

Let's start building that pyramid, from the bottom up of course, with ground training.

The concept of training from the ground isn't something new and exciting that I thought up all by myself. It has been well established for centuries, and is still widely valued and practised at the most well-respected centres of equestrianism in the world, such as the Spanish Riding School in Austria, the Cadre Noir in France and the Household Cavalry in Britain.

Although these establishments were originally established primarily for training war horses, it doesn't mean that their practices should be made redundant. I know that if I had to go to war on a horse, I wouldn't want one that wasn't balanced and obedient. Similarly, I wouldn't want to hack out a horse that had no brakes and steering on the roads of today, let alone compete on one. This is also one of the reasons so many of the principles I use here are also widely used by cowboys; they spend so much time with their horses, they couldn't afford to have them being disobedient all the time!

Now, ideally, all of these first basic steps would have been put in place before our horses were backed, but that is rarely the case. But if any of you has a nice unbacked youngster waiting to be started, you can use this process of halter training and long-lining, before you even think of backing him. For the rest of you, it's never too late.

Training: Level 1

Four-directional control
and ground training

*Ground training is made up of three areas:
halter work, rope-circling work and long-lining.*

This book is not intended to provide a step-by-step guide to each of these elements, which are covered in detail in my previous book *Unlock Your Horse's Talent* (David & Charles, 2003). However, I do intend to show how these processes lead to more advanced work, since the aim of this book is to give you tools that you can use to improve your horse's way of going. Later I talk about lateral work, and its place and importance in any horse's training regime, whether you are hacking out or competing (see pages 130–142). The key to success in lateral work is gaining control over your horse's body in every direction through ground training.

Ground training allows you to direct and control each of the four quarters of the horse – that is, the left and right shoulders, and left and right hind feet. I call this four-directional control, and it is important because:

1. It gives you the ability to break down problems and evasions into smaller pieces, which increases your chances of success

2. It allows you to be clear to your horse which leg or quarter you are correcting or directing

3. It helps you to isolate and work on specific issues such as stiffness and lack of dexterity

4. It teaches your horse to move his feet logically and not emotionally

Driving
line

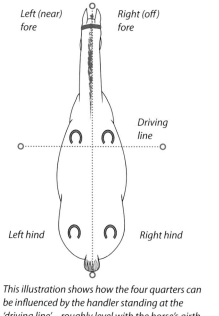

Left (near)
fore

Right (off)
fore

Driving
line

Left hind

Right hind

This illustration shows how the four quarters can be influenced by the handler standing at the 'driving line' – roughly level with the horse's girth – while doing groundwork. You can 'drive' any part of the horse in any direction.

EQUIPMENT

1. Training halter

I prefer to use a training halter that applies and releases pressure. The speed at which the halter releases is of utmost importance, which is why I use an 8mm braid-on-braid yachting rope, which is very smooth and won't snag on itself. Once the horse is listening to me I will use an ordinary horseman's halter; if I start with one of these, I often find the horse's response times are slower. I don't use a normal headcollar as they don't give the required control, and I find that many horses have become unresponsive and ignorant towards them.

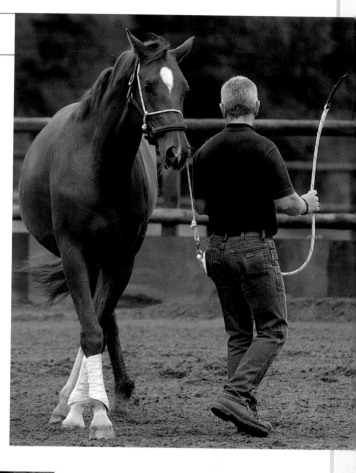

2. Rope

I use a 4m (12ft) rope with a leather tassel on the end. The tassel isn't to make the rope look pleasing but to give me an option for tactile pressure from a distance. When I want to do more advanced work I use a 7m (22ft) rope, again with a tassel on the end.

3. Long lines

For long-lining I use a pair of 10m (32ft) webbed lines. They are longer than normal lunge lines to allow for the longer outside line. I also use a fillet string or an old stirrup leather to secure the stirrups together under the horse's girth.

There are two rein positions that I use when long-lining, depending on how advanced the horse is in his training; these are shown on page 94. For the more advanced rein setting (position two), you need a pair of double-ended clips and two large rings.

Sarah Pyke and Dan

Max:

One of the key things I have learnt over the last few years is that what appears to be a problem between horse and rider is not the real problem at all, but a red herring! It just happens to be the point at which the relationship between horse and rider finally breaks down, creating an issue upon which they have both become fixated. A bit of investigation usually reveals that the true problem lies elsewhere, in a lack of trust or respect which goes much deeper.

For example, take a horse that doesn't like going through water or jumping ditches. I see lots of these, and usually it's got nothing to do with the ditch itself. The ditch is just the catalyst that sets off an emotional pattern of behaviour in the horse, a chain reaction that we must help him overcome. After all, how many of us react hysterically towards a hairy spider in the bath, knowing full well that there is no way these tiny fragile creatures can possibly cause us any physical harm?

As horse trainers, it's vitally important for us to realize that going out there and making the horse focus on the ditch itself will make matters worse. It's the equivalent of someone picking up that spider, putting it down your neck and telling you to just get used to it! Instead, we need to re-introduce rational behaviour and logical decision-making into the equation, getting the horse to focus on us rather than the object of his fear.

To do this successfully, you must be meticulous in your preparation. Trying to build on wobbly foundations is a guaranteed recipe for disaster, so before you even think

1 The first step is getting Dan to listen to the halter. Just because he is good at groundwork doesn't mean he is going to jump the ditch first time. He wants to know whether we are as committed to making him do it as he is to avoiding it!

2 Once he is responding to the halter, I put myself on the other side of the ditch and get Dan to jump towards me, so he has to come forwards to release the pressure. Although he jumps it, he still isn't sure about it, so this is the time for lots of praise and practice. Horses in this excited state can make unpredictable leaps, so always keep yourself safe and think about your personal space. The 22-foot line provides plenty of it. Once Dan has jumped the ditch a few times he gains his confidence and really starts to improve.

about tackling any problems, your horse must be firmly established in his groundwork and have the first base of the training pyramids, set in stone. This not only gives him the best possible chance of understanding, but also gives you the best chance of succeeding, since horses under pressure often want to put their handler to the test and see how committed you are.

In a few difficult cases, horses will throw every trick in the book at you, but just as you are starting to doubt your judgement and think you can't keep it up, so are they! Stick it out for a further few minutes, and they generally feel that the trick has failed and abandon the tantrum.

Thoroughbred gelding Dan is Sarah's first horse. I first met him as a loading problem. Since Sarah is now able to load him successfully, she has been out and about getting quite good marks in dressage, and decided that she would like to event. However, Dan's first few hunter trials revealed that he lacked confidence at cross-country, and he refused to jump ditches, water and any other strange-looking fences.

Because Dan had already learnt the principles of pressure and release from our loading sessions, my work on this occasion was a bit easier. When teaching a horse something new, especially when problems are anticipated, I always get the rider off his back. That way, the horse can make his mistakes and learn from them without the additional burden of a rider's weight, and without being able to blame the rider for his predicament! I also start slowly. A horse can jump a small fence (and of course you are going to start very small) from a standstill if necessary, so why canter a horse at a fence you know is going to cause problems? If you were learning to ballroom dance you wouldn't start by doing the dance at high speed; you would walk it through first to develop your technique and learn the steps.

We hired a cross-country course and made sure we had all the time and equipment we needed.

3 Once Dan is jumping the ditch with complete confidence on the line, we get Sarah back on board. Dan is still attached to the line to help him make the link between the previous dismounted exercise and what is expected of him now, and so that Sarah can experience the situation without having to think about the controls.

Some riders might worry that riding a horse over cross-country fences with a halter and a 22-foot line makes them look different, since most people try and sort out jumping problems by themselves from on top. But if you get the results you want, who cares? Remember you're not just your horse's rider but also his trainer, and as such you must do whatever helps him to best understand what is required of him with minimum stress.

4 Finally, we achieve a bold and confident jump off the line, showing that both horse and rider have overcome their fears and gained trust in each other. Sarah said afterwards that seeing Dan jump the ditch without a rider made her realize how bold he really was, which in turn gave her greater confidence. A few weeks later they entered and won a local hunter trial! So just one morning of work devoted to tackling this problem resulted in long-term progress, and from now on Sarah won't have to walk every new cross-country course in trepidation and worry about what lies ahead.

An introduction to halter training

The first step of the first step, as it were, is halter training.

If a horse uses evasions to take control of situations, I always start by using a training halter. The reason for this is that while a horse may initially only show one level of the evasion, he usually has a second level in reserve which gives him the confidence to use that negative behaviour in the first place. Halter work levels the playing field, so to speak, in that it cancels out the horse's belief that he is bigger, quicker and stronger than any person he comes across. If we can convince him of this then we can take charge again. Of course, in reality we will never be bigger, quicker and stronger than a horse, but using a halter is the most humane way I have found to change a horse's behaviour without them falling out with us, their rider/handler. I call it kidology.

If you haven't got a problem horse, halter training is still something you will need to do to successfully implement the next section of the book; areas of potential trouble which you didn't know existed might also be unearthed by ground training. They may not have culminated in a confrontation yet, but they will always be there to surprise and undermine you if you don't sort them out now.

The key here is to teach your horse to move away from pressure and to come forwards off pressure. Once he does this well, you can move on to lateral work from the ground. You will have already tried backing up your horse early on (page 40); now you need to teach him to come forwards off the pressure.

REFRESHER COURSE FOR FERDI

Ferdi is very clever and has everyone around him doing things the way he likes them, and as long as everyone complies he is a really nice horse – but he definitely doesn't like to be challenged. He is a nice horse to be around, and is curious and cheeky, but he is about to be found out, as you will see on the following pages. I haven't seen him for several years and my methods of training were different then, so he has never been put in these situations before. (For some of Ferdi's history see pages 90–91.)

First, some preparation for handling the halter and rope.

If you are going to ride after you have done some groundwork, there is no reason not to put the tack on and fit the halter over the bridle. Make sure your reins and stirrups are secure.

When using the rope and halter do not hold the rope from below, as shown (below left), but from above (below right) because if your wrist is uppermost a horse can unbalance you, whereas having it downwards gives you stability.

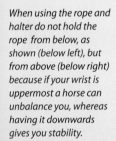

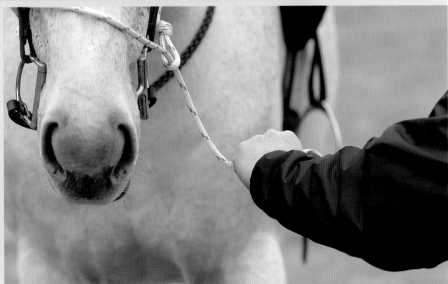

The first time he is asked to back up, Ferdi's offside ear is forward and the near ear is firmly on me (above). This tells me that I have his attention.

We can now start to move from the obvious to the subtle. Ferdi will now back up with a much softer hand (below).

1 Ferdi has started to get the measure of what is going on and doesn't really want to submit to backing up. I am starting to find him out, as under that nice exterior is a very strong-willed character. He is dropping his head to avoid moving back.

2 Ferdi is also reluctant to come forwards off the pressure. Remember it is not about force. Take up a contact and maintain that contact, but do not yank or pull. If your horse starts to move backwards walk with him, maintaining the same level of pressure.

3 Ferdi has realized nothing is going to change until he does as he is asked: he starts to move back nicely.

4 Ferdi is starting to believe I mean what I say and is really getting the hang of it. He has learnt not to let the rope go tight and comes forwards beautifully. With a horse as bright and strong-willed as this, the only way to maintain progress and get the best out of him is to practise regularly and be very persistent.

1 **2**

3 **4**

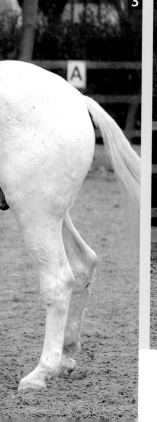

Circling work

When training any horse for any job, no matter what system you are using, a circle will always play a part in developing the horse's way of going. With this in mind I felt I had to come up with a way of working with a horse on a circle that was interesting to all parties. I don't know about you but I have always found lungeing very boring, and if I find it dull, then I can be sure the horse does too. I have noticed that after three times round on a circle a horse switches off, so you have to either change direction or pace to keep the horse's focus truly on you.

As with everything I do, I start off using very obvious signals and work towards becoming more subtle. Using this process develops balance and self-carriage, and enables you to take control of the shoulders and of the quarters on the move.

Within just a few minutes of starting, I have this mare's full attention. Look at her left ear registering my command for her to move in that direction. I signal what I want by applying visual pressure to her right shoulder through swinging the rope (this can be backed up with tactile pressure with the end of the rope on her shoulder if she fails to respond) while indicating that the 'door' is open to allow her movement to the left.

OK, so we get another over-reaction. At least it shows that the mare is watching me very carefully now, ready to spring into action at my slightest command. Since I am staying calm and neither punishing nor rewarding her for this behaviour, she will soon work out that she is the only one working hard here, and that she is actually making life difficult for herself! This is simply another form of evasion and it will get her nowhere.

Secure in the knowledge that the mare understands the concept of pressure and release, I apply pressure to the line to draw her head to me, which naturally has the effect of sending her quarters away. Compare this to the wilful display in the second picture. Now the mare's demeanour is much more humble and she is really concentrating on me. Even though I am several feet away, she is careful not to allow the rope to tighten while waiting for her next instruction. Note that when I reward her, I will bring her to me by shortening the line, not by walking towards her.

Altogether calmer, the mare has quickly learnt that there was no benefit in the decision to run she made earlier. Note also that there is no tension in the line. Horses quickly become so attuned to avoiding pressure on the halter that you should be able to circle them just with fingertips. This is the beginning of teaching them self-balance, as well as obedience from a distance; this mare is learning not to lean, a concept she will eventually carry through to her ridden work.

Jo Sharples and Ferdinand

Jo:

Ferdinand is a 17.3hh Warmblood gelding, originally bred for great things in the dressage world, but – to cut a long story short – the intensity of the training turned him very sour and by the age of five he was already ruined. He may have looked the part, but mentally and emotionally he just wasn't cut out for life in a big competition yard and ended up with Max as a 'problem horse'.

The most serious of these problems was napping, which had escalated into a rearing habit, which he used to avoid leaving the yard or entering a dressage arena. Although several very experienced riders had tried various tactics to 'show him who was boss', he proved to be a stronger character than any of them, and simply reared higher until they gave up on him.

At the time, I had a nice young horse on loan from Max, so when he called me to say that my 'new horse' had just arrived in the yard and he wanted to do a swap I wasn't too keen! After all, I was just an average Riding Club fun rider, what did I want with a rearing prima donna? But Max had done the hard work for me, sorting out the physical pain that had been the cause of Ferdinand's bad behaviour, and getting him to find the forward gears again by using lots of groundwork and the wip-wop (see page 96) in his ridden work.

By the time I met him six weeks after his arrival at Max's place, Ferdi was just a grumpy, disillusioned creature who needed some tender loving care and a one-to-one relationship with an undemanding rider to rebuild his shattered ego. In fact, what he really needed was to forget the posh dressage stuff in which he had been drilled every day of his life and to have some fun, so for the first few months we hacked, jumped, galloped around the countryside and generally did everything but dressage.

I can honestly say I never had any serious problems with him from the first day. He was still very opinionated and inclined to get a bit nappy, but a quick flick from the wip-wop soon reminded him to go forwards, and as long as I continued religiously with the groundwork at home we were fine. I rode him out with the halter under his bridle and a rope in my pocket and if I ever felt worried, I simply dismounted and started doing some halter work with him there and then! One day it had been so long since he had shown any sign of a problem, I decided to take him into an arena and see how he behaved; riding a horse that had been trained to such an advanced level was a revelation, and I swear he loved every minute of showing me how clever he was.

The more I got to know him, the more I realized that the root of Ferdi's apparent stubbornness was in fact huge sensitivity. Even nine years later, he still gets highly offended if anyone gives what he judges to be a 'rude' aid. All those early lessons when he was highly schooled to seat and weight aids mean he is a fantastic (although unforgiving) teacher. I get constant feedback from him about every movement of my body and every aid I give – whether I know I'm giving it or not! When I block him by being tight or out of balance anywhere, mentally or physically (this can be as subtle as clenching my jaw, wearing unsuitable clothing such as thick bulky gloves or simply being a bit absent-minded after a long day at work), he just stops dead and swishes his tail, refusing to go forwards. I have to work through my whole body eliminating any tension, getting control of my movements and thinking myself into the right frame of mind before I can get anywhere with him. When I concentrate on staying soft and manage to keep my part of the bargain, he does too; it's like riding by telepathy.

The result of having such a complex character to deal with is that I have been on a steep learning curve since day one, and am on a constant mission to develop body awareness and greater subtlety. He is the horse of a lifetime, and getting to grips with him has sent me down roads I didn't even know were on the map in the search for answers. It all happened so gradually I can't recall any defining moments when he turned from 'bad' to 'good', until at shows people started to tell me how lucky I was to have such a quiet, well-mannered horse! Nine years later and the groundwork remains a critical part of my regime, and although his behaviour no longer necessitates it, I generally do some every day even if just for a few minutes.

What Max says about problems at the pinnacle of the pyramid disappearing when you rebuild the base is true to the absolute letter; Ferdi has not reared or misbehaved significantly once in all the time I have had him. Sure, he still has a half-hearted nap in him when he feels he'd like to express an opinion, but it is a token gesture and his cheek just makes me laugh. In fact, I rode him until I was eight and a half months pregnant and felt completely safe! It was only when people who knew the 'old Ferdi' expressed absolute horror at this that I realized how far we'd come.

From problem horse to a mount safe enough for pregnancy! Jo Sharples, who was the project editor on this book, with Ferdi at the photoshoot.

Long-lining
(working on a circle with two reins)

I find long-lining absolutely necessary in any horse's training, and one of the first misconceptions I would like to change is that long-lining is difficult. It isn't, although it does take practice to get comfortable, but that's only because it is something new. If you have the dexterity to ride a horse and a bike and drive a car, then you have the skills to be able to long-line. It is a very efficient tool that can help to change many things about your horse, and it is also very interactive.

PHYSICAL BENEFITS OF LONG-LINING

The primary aspect of riding is that your horse must carry your weight efficiently through all paces, changes of direction and gymnastic movements. The more we can prepare for this during ground training the better and easier it will be for the horse. Long-lining improves the horse in the following ways:

1. Engagement. The horse learns to push himself forwards from behind, stepping further underneath his body to further support his back against the weight of the rider.

2. Suppleness. This means that you don't get a locked-up and stiff ride from your horse. If he is stiff and locked up, he will find work difficult, uncomfortable and, in severe cases, will be in pain.

3. Self-motivation. It is the horse's responsibility to carry himself, but you have to set it up so that all of the above elements come into play and allow your horse to carry himself correctly. Without the weight of a rider, he will learn to go forwards happily and readily, a lesson he will, hopefully, then take into his ridden work.

4. Straightness. Thanks to all of the above.

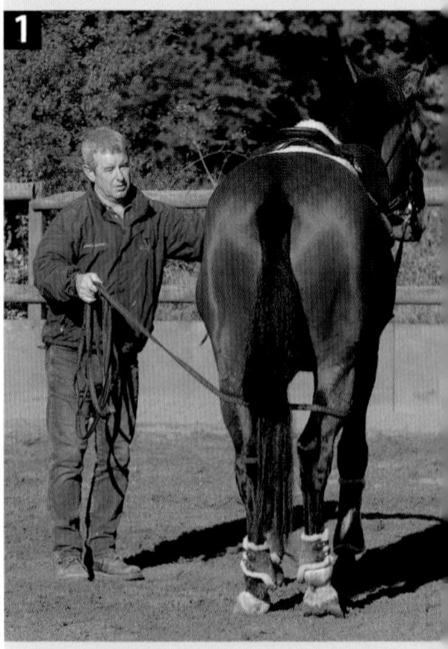

1 Start by standing on the nearside and put the line over his head and back and round his quarters. The idea is to get your horse used to the sensation of the line behind him, and to follow the feel of the line.

I love long-lining as it is so interactive – I can turn, change pace and move up and down the arena at will.

PREPARATION FOR LONG-LINING

Before you decide to long-line you need to know how your horse will react to having a line behind him.

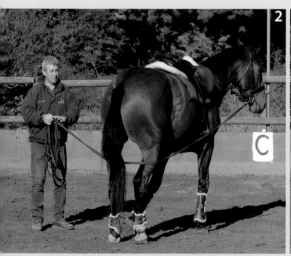

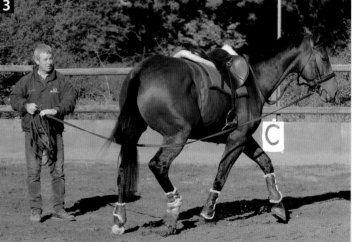

2 Take up a feel. You are asking your horse to move away from the pressure of that feel. As he moves off, collect up the slack created by the horse moving through himself, until he is facing you. Repeat until he confidently moves around and repeat on both reins.

3 Although this exercise is primarily used for preparation of long-lining it also creates a lot of flexibility in the horse. Note how Jo moves his near foreleg; he has picked it up and crossed it over in front of the opposite foreleg, showing great flexibility.

POSITION ONE
(novice)

Position one is the foundation of long-lining, allowing the horse to move comfortably and gradually find a good working shape. The long lines pass from the bit through the stirrup iron, which has been secured with an old stirrup leather.

When securing your stirrup irons make sure they do not bang your horse's elbows: have them about 10cm (4in) above the point of the elbow.

It may take several attempts to get your horse moving nicely on the lines, so don't get disheartened if it takes a while. You are aiming for your horse to have nice even, regular paces.

POSITION TWO
(advanced)

For position two, the long lines pass from the bit through rings attached to the saddle and back down to the stirrup iron. This position will give you a more advanced outline, lightening the forehand by getting your horse to use his quarters more efficiently. Never start a training session in position two; always do around 15 minutes in position one and no more than a further 20 minutes in position two.

For position two the black web strap sits over the withers and is attached to the D rings on the front of the saddle with the loose rings either side of the horse for the lines to pass through.

In position two you can get your horse to become very dynamic, elevated and flowing. I love this photo of Jo as it shows an excellent weight-carrying posture and also it shows me how fantastic he has become!

CHANGING DIRECTION

Don't panic if it takes time to become proficient at changing direction. Practise at walk, and before you know it you will be able to change direction at speed with a fluid action. Bear in mind where your hands would be if you were riding; do not lift your hands too high, and move them down the lines to maintain a steady contact.

On the right rein, notice that both lines are in my right hand, while my left hand runs down the outside line as far as I can reach.

As the horse feels the outside line tighten and starts to change direction, open your right hand and allow the momentum and the movement of the horse to take the line through your hand. Once your horse is back on the circle going to the left, your hands should be back in the position you were in before asking for a change of direction.

CORRECT HAND POSITION

Long-lining is riding from the ground, so you need to have your hands in a similar position to that of riding.

This is not a good position to be in with your hands (above), but happens quite often when you are new to long-lining. Always have in the back of your mind 'Would I ride with this hand position?' Even when I am adjusting the lines (below), my hands are low.

Rachel and Mog

Rachel:

I was a horse-mad kid with totally non-horsey parents, so I had to be satisfied with a weekly lesson and as much time as I could spend down at the local riding stables. From the time I got my first horse when I was 18, I was blessed with easy-to-do types with no hang-ups, and had a brilliant time. It wasn't until I got my present horse, Mr McGonagal (known as Mog), that my handling and riding knowledge was put to the test.

Mog, a shy Irish cob, came to me as an unsure four-year-old. He was initially extremely headshy but we slowly worked through this. I had lessons to begin with, and all went well. We hacked out and Mog gained confidence … then slowly he developed the 'stop', which he put into good use whenever he felt like it. Going in and out of the stable, leading, riding, and loading in the trailer, you name it, he would plant his feet and refuse to move.

Max:

Mog was clever enough to use one evasion to cover a multitide of situations, keeping it simple but effective!

Rachel:

I asked advice, talked to experts and delved back into my memory for something which might help. Overall the general consensus was that I was too soft with him, and needed to 'show him who is boss'. Spurs and schooling whips were suggested and in my ignorance I allowed various trainers to try their techniques on Mog, but each time I knew after one session that this was not the answer. I also knew in my heart that Mog was a genuine horse and it was up to me to find a better way of communicating with him.

Flicking through a horsey catalogue, I found a book written by Max called *Unlock Your Horse's Talent* (David & Charles 2003). I had always been interested in his techniques so I ordered it. When I say that I read it twice from cover to cover, I honestly mean it. The more I read, the more I had a feeling that this might be the beginning of a highly acceptable way of dealing with all of Mog's issues, so I ordered a training halter and explanatory DVD. Within a couple of sessions of halter

work, I noticed that Mog was more polite at the stable door and when tied up.

Then I began the rope circling to gain control of his quarters. Progress was slow mainly due to my inexperience but gradually Mog began to move away to only a small turn of the rope and started to sharpen up generally to the technique; but we had a long way to go. I still had problems when ridden, leading in-hand at shows and loading in the trailer and when ridden. Mog would still stop for no apparent reason. I made myself an 'over-and-under' (or wip-wop) from an old headcollar rope (minus the clip) and this proved a useful aid in getting him to move forwards, but he would still misbehave out hacking and at shows.

Over-and-under (wip-wop) in use.

Max:

An over-and-under is used to create forward movement. It is inspired by those old Westerns we have all seen, where the cowboys ride out of town at great speed, flicking their reins over one side of the saddle then the other. When using one for the first time, it is always advisable to have a neckstrap so that if your horse shoots forwards you don't catch him in the mouth.

Rachel:

Clearly, I needed some one-to-one tuition. I took the plunge and phoned Max. The first obvious difference when

Max did the halter work was the increase in speed of Mog's reactions. Suddenly, my laid-back little Irish cob lightened up and began to move his feet and respond in a way I had never seen before.

Max:

This is mainly because of my experience with using the rope (over-and-under). My request for forward movement was very clear to Mog. This is rather like someone talking to a foreigner in their own language. If you don't get it quite right, it may take the foreigner a while to work out what is being said, even if you string the basic words together correctly.

When you are working your horse look for licking and chewing, as it is indicative of submission, but it is also a reaction to the horse thinking.

Rachel:

Max worked methodically through the four-directional control techniques and rope circling, and explained that Mog's 'stop and plant tactic' was a highly effective evasion that required little effort on his part! With regular four-directional halter work, Mog soon gave up on this and was frequently seen 'chewing many thoughts over' in his head.

Max then applied the halter work to Mog's trailer-loading issues. Again, the 'stop' was Mog's trump card, but Max worked him through this using the halter and within around 20 minutes he was loading without any hesitation. I also learned an important lesson, which was not to slam the ramp up in relief the first time you get a difficult loader to comply. If the load is not perfect and there is any hesitation, it must be repeated – and this even goes for show mornings. It only took me a moment to realize that a few seconds' hesitation on day one, if not rectified at the time, could build up to minutes and hours as the show season progressed.

Max then introduced Mog to long-lining and explained its advantages over one-line lungeing to me. My main feeling when lungeing Mog was that I always seemed to be doing more work that he was. Long-lining would put the emphasis back on Mog doing the work, as well as giving me a new way of teaching him, improving my own co-ordination and seeing exactly how Mog moved.

The final session involved some ridden work. Max showed me how to use the over-and-under correctly

and stressed that I should always ask Mog to move forwards with the lightest of leg aids first, then if there is no response, use the over-and-under, but not to use my leg aid as well. This way Mog would learn that my leg aid was the softer option and more importantly, he would respond to a much lighter aid, giving me a much easier ride.

The 'residual Max effect' lasted about a week. I did my halter work and other exercises each evening and I found it quite easy to improve my techniques. But after about a week, Mog's responses slowed a bit. I went back to the video of the session and began to notice the subtleties of Max's body language and also where he stood when applying the pressure (whether it was at the shoulders or quarters) and I realized that perhaps I was not fully adopting the 'say what you mean, mean what you say' approach (see pages 28–29). So I really concentrated on these important points and gradually Mog sharpened up again and actually began to show an improvement after each session.

Max:

No horse is ever totally 'cured' of certain tendencies, and you have to keep the schooling up to scratch and be prepared for the horse to test you from time to time, no matter how well you are doing your homework. I think we can get stuck into thinking that it should always be perfect, but horses are no different to us really – no matter how good you are at your job, there will be times when you simply can't be bothered. I think it's crucial that people remain realistic. Horses aren't robots that can be programmed to perform in an identical manner every time.

Rachel:

However, the loading ceased to be a problem from that day on. I always do five minutes preparatory halter work first, just to get Mog listening, and if the load is not perfect I have developed the self-discipline to get him out and do it again. Five months later this rarely happens and we can now leave the showground with everyone else! Meanwhile, the effect the long-lining has had on his ridden work is quite amazing. Mog now has a purposeful walk, has slowly begun to muscle up in all the right places and looks a different cob. And it's so enjoyable, it doesn't seem like work!

Developing dexterity

If you can ride a horse and drive a car, you can definitely develop the dexterity you need to tackle this groundwork effectively. Many people are particularly reluctant to long-line, but you will be stuck on the first rung of the training ladder for ever if you don't make an effort to master it. This is where we need to stop and think about what it is we expect from our horses and then take a look at ourselves. We want our horses to work equally well on each rein, yet we don't write with both hands, and won't have a go at long-lining.

I grew up thinking that I was left-handed, and I definitely always felt more comfortable using my left hand for many things, although I write with my right

hand. I also feel as though I have equal strength in my left and right sides, so I think I do lean towards being ambidexterous, which is probably why I find working horses quite easy.

I did feel a little disadvantaged about this when I was growing up because everyone used to try and make me use my right hand more, especially when I was using a knife and fork. Interestingly, one of my sons uses his knife and fork the 'wrong' way round, but I haven't said anything to him. I want him to do whatever is comfortable.

Practise your rope skills before you try them out on your horse. For example, if you are worried about spinning a rope, tie it to a fence and try spinning it with one hand and then the other, until you can do it well with either hand. Remember to spin over-arm, not under-arm.

The real challenge to my dexterity came when I broke my right arm quite severely while trying to back a horse, and had to have it pinned. I was in plaster for 12 weeks, with ten horses in livery and no staff, so I just had to get on with it. It was really hard at first as I hadn't been using my left arm as much as I thought, but after a few weeks I found that I could muck out, long-line and do pretty much everything with my left hand almost as well as my right. When I came out of plaster I was amazed at how truly ambidextrous I had become.

Now I'm not saying that you have to go and break your arm to improve your dexterity, but I would like you to be more aware of how little you really do use the arm that is less dominant, and how making yourself practise will improve things.

Try juggling, or do that old trick of rubbing your tummy and patting your head at the same time, then quickly do it in reverse. Instead of using the arm that comes naturally for everyday things, such as grooming or shaving, make yourself use the other one.

After all, if you can't work equally on both reins, then why should your horse?

ROUND PENS AND LONG-LINING

If you have a round pen then only use it to get started when long-lining. Once you have the hang of it, come out of the round pen into an open field or arena, as I have found that horses that only work in the pen become dependent on the pen walls and the results are not the same.

MAXIMIZE YOUR HORSEMANSHIP

Max's regime
Half the pressure, double the effect?

In the ideal world, it would be great if we could all spend two or three hours a day at the yard looking after our horses, but the reality is that most of us have other commitments, which is why careful planning and use of the pyramid is essential.

You may be surprised to learn that I no longer have a yard of my own; I spend a lot of time travelling up and down the country helping owners and riders with their horses at their own yards, which means that I have to fit my horses in and around my job, just like everybody else. I also have a family, and three sons who like to play football and get involved in as many other sports as possible. So bearing all that in mind I have to be realistic about what I can achieve in the time available. This year I have been able to do a number of one-day events, which is something I have wanted to do for years, but had thought was impossible because I work away from home a lot and on weekends I want to spend time with my family. It was very hard to get a balance, or so I thought, until my wife Sam got fed up and said if I spent as much time planning as I did moaning I would probably get a lot more done!

Planning is not one of my stronger points, but I realized that I was never going to achieve anything with my own horse if I didn't put something together. There was my wonderful horse Jo standing idle, and I was feeling very dissatisfied. I could only guarantee to be at the livery yard where Jo is kept on a Friday, Saturday and Sunday, as I don't work on those days and am generally at the other end of the country for the rest of the week. This made my dream of eventing very difficult, especially when it came to keeping up the horse's fitness. I soon realized that I needed some help, so I did something that I never thought I would do, and looked for someone to share my horse.

I put out a plea for rider who had the ability to event at novice level but didn't have a horse to ride. I got only one reply, from a New Zealander called Cindy who lived over an hour away. She came down to the yard to meet myself and Jo, and it went really well, but I felt the distance would cause a problem. However, Cindy said she would rather travel for an hour to ride a nice horse for free than drive for an hour to ride a horse she had to pay for, which I thought was a good philosophy! That was in the spring of 2004 and she is still riding Jo. Without her I wouldn't be able to do half of the things I'm doing.

Now I have someone making sure that Jo's basic fitness is up to scratch, I can spend the three days I have putting in the schooling, which changes according to his competition schedule. Cindy rides two to three times a week and on top of that Jo goes on the horsewalker once or twice a day for 30 minutes. This is mainly because turnout space is limited, as it is in many yards, especially in winter, and at least with the horsewalker sessions plus hacking he gets a few extra hours out of his box. It isn't ideal but we all have to live with whatever facilities are available.

On Fridays I generally do some groundwork, since Jo has already had plenty of hacking out and fitness work. He is quite advanced in his groundwork so I work him in position two on the long lines which makes his workout a little more aerobic without him having to carry the weight of the rider, and prepares him for the next day's training with saddle and rider.

Saturday is when I generally do a bit of jumping or practise my dressage test. This will be quite a hard session physically and sometimes emotionally too, if I have been working on something new. Often at the end of the session we will go out for a hack, mainly in walk, just to have a wind down.

On Sunday, I may go over what I have done the day before if it was new, so that I can start to habituate the right responses. If not I will do a long slow period of schooling, working on the finer details in walk to enable Jo to absorb the information. Doing most of the session in walk allows Jo to unwind physically, before he hacks out with Cindy over the next few days to unwind mentally. I am also a big fan of loose schooling if you have a safe environment. It is a really good way of interacting with your horse from the ground without any equipment, and I quite often put up a fence and loose jump too. I also frequently use the Equissage machine (see page 63) on Jo. I believe this has huge mental and physical benefits.

As for the family, well, on a Friday I get to have a lie-in as I've normally done a 50-hour week by Thursday night, then I always make sure I pick up the boys from school. At the weekend I make sure that I'm up early so that I can get everything done by lunchtime, and I have the rest of the day to spend with the family. Looks like my father-in-law was right about planning all along!

Jo came to me as a horse that was dangerous – implementing this system we are now out and about competing.

Chapter 4

USING AND IMPROVING YOUR NEW SKILLS

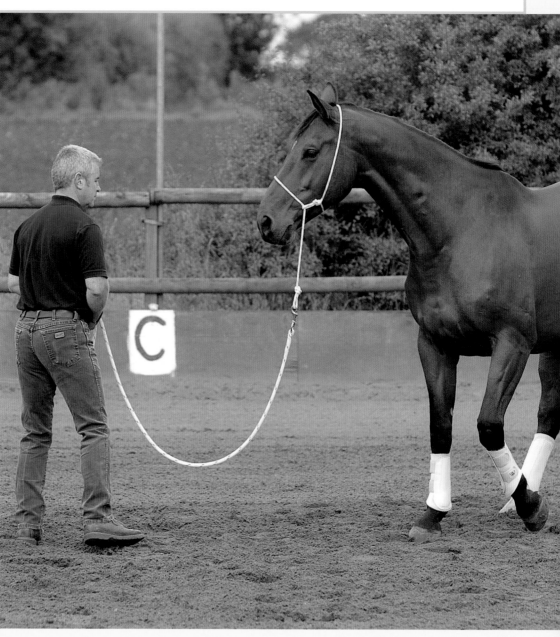

Training: Level 1

The groundwork described in the previous chapter is so challenging and versatile, it can be taken to a level where it is almost an end in itself; but let's not forget that this book is all about learning how to train your horse to improve his ridden performance.

The groundwork will help you achieve this directly by keeping the horse physically sound and able to perform, but you are training the horse's mind as much as his body, and the groundwork will help with this, too.

It is important to understand how the horse's brain works, what exercises you can use to help him learn, and how you can keep his focus and attention on you, even in situations he finds exciting. In fact, it's so important that it is a keystone in the foundation of your training pyramid, so let's go into more detail.

Left- and right-brain thinking

Most mammals have two functionally distinct brain hemispheres. The left brain hemisphere is the logically cognitive, interactive, analytical and communicative part of the brain, while the right brain hemisphere governs emotion, feeling and reactivity.

Humans generally use both sides of the brain to a greater or lesser degree, depending on the situation; we are able to use either logical reasoning or adrenalin-fuelled instinct as a response to varying circumstances.

Left brain is

logically cognitive
interactive
analytical
communicative

Right brain governs

emotion
feeling
reactivity

Horses have survived as a species by relying heavily on the right side of their brain, which is where they have most of their instinctive and emotional responses; anger, fear and confusion are all part of right-brain thinking. The horse's brain is hard-wired to automatically react and respond to danger without hesitation. The only trouble is, his idea of danger and yours might be very different!

It is crucial to know how the horse's brain works when put under the pressure of being trained or retrained. Many of the things we do with our domesticated horses require them to over-rule their natural instincts, and so we need to ask in such a way as to gain control without destroying their individuality, which makes them the horses we love.

Emotionally, most horses work just below the point of being out of control. As I said above, a horse is not designed to think logically in a crisis, but to respond to his environment and to react accordingly. This requires adrenalin, which fuels the horse's ability to block out logical thinking and run with his instincts. It's quick, effective and life-saving on the wide open plains when you don't have much thought-time in an emergency, but not much use in the average livery yard where predators are few and far between.

Through domestication and training we are trying to reverse this process so that the horse will use the left side of his brain – the analytical, thinking side – rather than reacting emotionally. When a horse uses the left side of his brain, he releases endorphins, which have a calming effect and block the flow of adrenalin. Once a horse gets used to doing this, he will become much happier in his training, more co-operative and easier to train. It also means you have a horse that is safer in unexpected situations.

Horses have survived as a species by relying heavily on the right side of their brain, where they have most of their instinctive and emotional responses; anger, fear and confusion are all part of right-brain thinking.

The switch from left to right

Horses go into self-preservation mode instinctively and immediately over all kinds of things. Often, just having a dog shoot out unexpectedly or hearing a lorry rattle past in the distance can be enough to set them off. While such behaviour may seem annoying and unnecessary to the handler of a jumpy horse, we must remember that it is this highly developed instinct that has kept the horse alive for so many thousands of years. Without it, he would have become extinct long ago, so no wonder he finds it hard to give up, even in the safety of his own stable!

Some horses have a more highly developed sense of flight than others, but one thing all horses have in common is that when they do react in this way, the right side of the brain has taken over. This is the part that governs their emotional response to perceived danger and activates that 'flight or fight' instinct which is so highly developed in horses. When this happens, there's a kind of short-circuit of the more logical, left side of the brain, and that 'lights-are-on-but-nobody's-home' expression appears on your horse's face as he stares into the distance!

When the horse is in this state of heightened awareness and excitement, his logical reasoning cannot work effectively at the same time. To overcome this we need to use a training process that will cause

Some horses have a more highly developed sense of flight than others, but one thing all horses have in common is that when they do react in this way, the right side of the brain has taken over.

Mattie is really expressing himself. When this happens, it is vital that you, as the handler, stay calm and let the horse get it out of his system. It is no different to a dog having a 'mad moment'!

him to reconnect with his left brain, the thinking and analytical side. If we can keep this side active, he'll be less likely to panic or over-react, and we'll have the tools we need to get his concentration back when he is momentarily startled. Horses use the left side of the brain when they are asked to do school work such as lateral exercises because these require them to think about where they are putting their feet; backing up through the labyrinth (see photograph, below right) is another exercise that stimulates the use of the left side of the brain. Doing 15 minutes of lateral work beforehand is fantastic for calming a horse that gets overwrought while out on a hack, as it will release calming endorphins. Use the groundwork described in chapter 3 (pages 66–101) to form the broad base of your support; key ridden exercises follow in chapter 5.

MAXIMIZE YOUR HORSEMANSHIP

Some right-brain management concepts

To overcome the flight response, the handler or rider must establish himself as the leader in the mind of the horse; this is where your basic ground-training skills will come into play. Remember that a frightened horse is unable to learn, so no matter what reaction you get from your horse, when he perceives there is an emergency you must remain calm and passive until he has worked out that everything is all right. A horse can be taught to work through a situation and to follow the cues and aids of the rider in unfamiliar and threatening situations.

This is especially true when you are riding your horse in a situation where there is the potential for him to become worried. If you have trained him to listen to you and to use the left side of his brain, he is less likely to be dangerous. He is entitled to be a bit cautious, but not so worried that he takes control of the situation.

The more you ask your horse to use the left side of his brain, the more successful he will become at doing so, and his confidence will grow and he will use the right side of his brain less and less.

There will be points in your training where your horse will go slightly 'right-brained' (photograph, left), but I look at this as a stress release, not unlike the days when we need to go for a run or have a good cry to get rid of pent-up energy or emotion. We have to accept that training will generate some stress and that at some point the horse will have to relieve it. This doesn't mean we will accept the horse always responding unfavourably to stress, but just that we don't let it upset us and we work methodically to bring it under control with the exercises described.

The role of stress

A prey animal has to flee from danger, so when he sees, hears or smells something disconcerting it generates stress. This builds up his adrenalin levels and makes him physically and mentally prepared to react if the stressful stimulation continues or intensifies. That reaction can be one of two things: fight or flight, and a horse will always prefer flight where it is possible. The flight or fight response will continue until the stress is relieved and the horse can then return to a tranquil state. It is crucial behaviour for the horse to survive among predators.

One can think of the horse as having a 'stress tank' inside his right brain. Each horse has an individual rate in which he fills his tank. Each horse also has a means to naturally drain the tank. A horse that fills quickly and drains slowly might be described as hot or volatile, while a horse that fills slowly and empties readily may be considered cold or laid back. How a horse handles his stress tank is a product of genetics as well as experience.

While we can't change a horse's genetic predisposition, we can affect his life experiences so that he is less prone to fill his stress tank and more efficient at keeping it drained. When stress management is included in the training process (in the context of teaching the horse how to manage his stress) then the handler will usually see significant improvements in the horse's behaviour.

Gemma is riding Burt through some scary bags and umbrellas. The more you prepare your horse for all sorts of eventualities at home, the less stressful they are when encountered in unfamiliar surroundings.

Whenever a horse shows signs of getting upset, a solution is to do some simple exercises in walk.

MAXIMIZE YOUR HORSEMANSHIP

Stress management: a question of speed

When a horse is in self-preservation mode, he is operating primarily with his right brain (fight or flight instinct) and can't learn much. If we can stimulate his curiosity, he will use his left brain, and engage his thinking and learning apparatus. Fortunately for us, horses don't efficiently use both hemispheres at the same time, they flip from one mode to another. So if we can keep the thinking side active, a horse will be less likely to panic or become violent.

With this in mind, think about our main three paces: walk, trot and canter. Horses are able to think quite clearly in the calm states of halt and walk, but this thinking ability lessens in trot and becomes very difficult in canter. This is why you will find a lot of emotional training problems show up in canter, such as horses becoming fizzy or starting to buck.

Now think back to horses in the wild. They spend most of their day in walk, wandering around and grazing. General interaction will create a bit of trot but only for a short amount of time. If a horse is in canter or gallop, he is generally fleeing something – an instinctive reaction that is fuelled by adrenalin. As we have already mentioned, instinctive actions effectively block logical thought.

So whenever a horse starts to show signs of getting upset, a simple solution is to slow things back down to walk and re-engage the left brain with some simple exercises. When you do this, you can visibly see and feel him calming down, provided you actually take charge and give him some exercises to encourage left-brain thinking, rather than just sitting there hoping he will slow down and stay in walk.

Making sure your horse is completely familiar and competent at all the exercises in walk is essential for this strategy to work. He's got to feel as if he is in a comfort zone and on familiar territory, so when he is upset is not the time to try anything new.

The more comfortable your horse becomes with his work, the greater his ability to remain calm, even when the pace increases. With practice, you really can train your horse to think straight, even in canter, even though this is against all his natural instincts, so give him and yourself due credit for achieving it.

Charlie Knapp and Ellie

Charlie:

I first met Welton Free Spirit (Ellie) when she was offered to me on loan. She was presented to me fully tacked up to go straight around the Berks and Bucks Draghounds Cubhunter Trial, a course renowned for its awesome hedges and fences. She gave me a fabulous bold ride, and from that point onwards I totally fell for her. At that time, I was on the core training squad of the British Pony Eventing Team and my aim was the FEI Pony Eventing Trials the following spring. I knew that her reputation preceded her, but she was the sweetest-natured pony around the stable and so I duly ignored the warning bells.

Ellie went beautifully on the flat at home, but from the minute we arrived at an event, she would shake like a leaf and refuse to eat. When left on the lorry by herself, she would climb up the walls and stand on the tack locker, even on one occasion putting her head through the roof of the lorry and one foot through a window. She was difficult and bargy to tack up, and once off the lorry would run in circles, knocking me over if I tried to make any tack adjustments from the ground. During the first hunter trial we attended it took two people to walk her before and after the class.

As we ventured to one or two dressage competitions, a pattern appeared. Ellie would work in well, but as soon as she entered the arena she would tense up and the tension would peak when she was asked to walk or halt. She would start to tighten and jog, and then leap about and finally end up either rearing or throwing herself around. She always jumped extremely well and pulled herself into the prizes by virtue of this, but the dressage was a different matter. Although we pulled off a couple of reasonable tests there were a number where she finished at the bottom of the class and had judges diving for cover.

Everybody offered advice and we tried all manner of preparation – working her for hours, working her for minutes, lungeing her, trying to tire her before her tests. We also tried various feed supplements, but nothing helped. We were placed in the 2004 British Pony Eventing Championships, when Ellie pulled up nearly 30 places from near bottom after the dressage with her excellent jumping, but Ellie wouldn't eat throughout the whole five days and the selectors were increasingly distrustful of her consistency. I thought Ellie was hugely talented and badly wanted to prove all the critics wrong, but I had nothing left to offer in terms of resolving the situation, and the selectors agreed she had no future as a team pony.

A few days later, my mother told me she had made an appointment for Max to come and see Ellie. I was totally sceptical, but we owed it to Ellie to at least try this last option, and I really liked Max from the moment I met him. He worked quietly at getting to know Ellie in the stable and spent a long time examining her physically, then worked Ellie in the arena on a pressure halter.

It was a seemingly simple device but I have never seen Ellie react in such a way. She was a fighter! Max explained that he was just asking Ellie to submit and walk towards him as he put pressure on the lead rope, but she fought every inch of the way. He was so patient, and just stood in the arena while she threw herself about, reared and tried to lie down. Eventually, after what seemed like hours, she submitted and took a few Spanish steps towards him. He repeated the exercise several times until she was totally quiet and submissive when asked to go back or forwards.

Max:

It was immediately apparent that Ellie was an adrenalin junkie! She just didn't know how to relax. Submission at the initial halter training stage with her was a defining moment, and it did seem to take a relatively long time, but she was such a tough cookie that she really had to know that I wasn't up for negotiating at this point. In turn, she showed me that she was an intelligent pony, and that the next few months were not going to be easy for Charlie.

Charlie:

Max then lunged Ellie on the same halter and line, showing me how to bring her in and disengage the hindquarters using rope circling when she went too fast.

Max:

When we are taught to school our horses and ponies we are taught that we must engage the hindquarters, which is really important as this is the horse's engine. However, it is equally important to teach a horse how to disengage their quarters and effectively turn off the engine, which is especially important when the brakes fail or adrenalin takes over.

Charlie:

Max then worked Ellie on long lines. I had done this before, but had not asked so many questions of her. Eventually he asked me to ride her again and I was amazed straightaway by the difference I felt. For the first time ever, I actually had to use my leg to ask her to move forwards.

Max:

Long-lining helped Ellie to slow down and think. Her main evasion was speed, and she would shut down and fight the bit when asked to slow down. Every time she went too fast, we used lots of changes in direction to slow her down without pulling on her mouth. Eventually she worked out that as soon as she went too fast, we could interrupt and regain control of her quarters, although it took her about 40 minutes to settle her, due to her high levels of adrenalin. It is important for the handler to remain completely calm through this, and not join in with the adrenalin-fuelled behaviour, which is much easier to do when you're not actually riding the horse! The other factor is that every time she made a turn, the thought process involved created a momentary endorphic release (in other words, a switch from right- to left-brained thinking.)

Charlie:

Max explained that Ellie's problem stemmed from her inability to prevent the adrenalin flow that culminated in her behaviour, and that he had used the exercises to get her to use the part of her brain that deals with logic. Suddenly it all seemed to make sense – in the wild Ellie could run for hours on that adrenalin, giving up only when she either dropped dead from exhaustion or was eaten by a predator! No wonder my hours of working in had been a waste of time …

A few weeks later we went to a Core Squad training session where we were to ride the European Dressage Test for the GB selectors. Max kindly agreed to come and help me work in, and explained again that Ellie's problems weren't a time issue but a brain issue. He only worked Ellie in hand for a short while before the test, and by the time I got on it was as if she had been drugged or was very ill and I had to work really hard to ride an active test! Ellie was at last starting to think about what she was being asked to do. One of the most useful exercises that Max had taught me was to send Ellie into a number of quick turns on the forehand as soon as she started to tighten or rear in the halts or walks. This had amazing results in controlling the flow of adrenaline by using the analytical side of her brain, making her both physically and emotionally a much happier pony.

We spent the winter working away at Max's exercises and when we went to dressage shows, I stopped trying to cover Ellie's faults and actually took her on in the arena, making her spin if she started to tense up or fidget. Of course, we had many 'throw away' classes, but gradually we started to gain better marks with Ellie even being placed in some affiliated classes.

We had a slight setback when I took Ellie to a GB Core Squad training session with the selectors. We were working in a group, which is not really ideal for Ellie, and

the format didn't really allow me to include the work Max had taught me to settle her. By the end of the session I felt her adrenalin flow was back to its previous levels; on the one hand it was annoying that the training format couldn't be a little more flexible, but on the other, it confirmed to me once and for all that Max's methods were really the answer for Ellie. Another benefit was that Max decided to go a stage further, and taught me to lay Ellie on the floor when she became too tense to handle.

Max:

Ellie is one of the toughest cases that I have worked with, and her way of using adrenalin as a coping mechanism was very deep-rooted. Teaching her to lie down was not something I did lightly, and I only did it after working with her for four months.

Lying down has the effect of completely draining the horse of adrenalin just as if it were submitting to a predator; obviously it puts the horse in a very vulnerable position with the handler at the top of the pecking order, and is a huge test of trust. It is not something I would recommend to try at home and I have only ever used it in a few extreme cases before, mainly on stallions.

Charlie with Ellie, 'chilling-out'.

Charlie:

By the time the first Pony FEI Selection Trial came in March 2005, we had improved dramatically and we pulled off a beautiful dressage test to lie second after this phase! I knew the rest would be easy for her, and she flew the show jumping and cross-country to end up as the winner, and the only pony to finish on its dressage score. The selectors were astounded, and I can honestly say it was the greatest sense of achievement I have ever felt. Ellie went on to perform really good tests at her next two trials. She was also far more relaxed and even started to eat while we were away, and I felt that we could finish our season with our heads held high. I'm proud we persevered where some of the experts had told us to give up. Max's faith in our ability to overcome these problems and the techniques he shared was a life-changing experience for which I am eternally grateful.

Mind games for the trainer

So far we've placed a lot of emphasis on getting your horse fit and ready to perform better, but how about you? There are usually physical, mental and emotional issues to address in the trainer, too!

When I first arrive with a client I will ask what their problems are and what they have been doing to try and overcome them. It generally turns out that to solve their problem, they have been doing more of what they were doing before they had a problem, which could well have been what caused it in the first place! Several weeks or months further down the line with no improvement, they need help to break out of this vicious circle they have found themselves in.

You cannot solve a problem, whether ridden or handling, by doing more of the same. This is where your pyramid comes in, to help guide you out of the situation in a logical and progressive way.

Of course, the most crucial part of problem solving is recognizing that you have one in the first place. Only when you have been completely honest with yourself can you start to re-evaluate how you are going to deal with it. This period of reconditioning yourself is crucial if you are going to have any success in changing your horse's issues. If you're really honest, you may see some parallels between your horse's issues and your own. Don't be surprised if you have to go back to the beginning and change aspects of your behaviour before you can change those of your horse. The reason I say this is that often a rider/handler thinks that they only have to go back a little way in order to sort out the problems they are having, but the chances are the problem is much more deep-rooted than that. It probably started a long time ago with very small issues that the average owner would simply dismiss as normal behaviour for a horse.

Reconditioning is not unlike being on a diet; to be successful and have long-term results, you need to change your lifestyle completely, rather than just eat less for a short while. Likewise, if you want long-term results in your horse's behaviour, you will have to get to the root of the problem and be committed to changing his management. This is not some fad diet. If you are half-hearted or put your new skills into practice for a short while, then you will only get temporary results.

DO YOU NEED RECONDITIONING?

To be a truly effective trainer, your new habits and horsemanship skills need to become second nature, so that they come into play each and every time you are with a horse. To see how well you are doing so far with your own horse, it can be helpful to make a chart, and give yourself a score ranging from zero to ten for a number of everyday handling scenarios. For it to work, you have to be really honest, and include situations along the following lines:

1. **Leading**

   If it is poor and your horse is rude, too slow or too fast, score between zero and three.

   If your horse leads at the same pace as you walk and doesn't pull, and is relatively obedient, score between four and eight.

   If he leads beautifully and also backs up and moves over when asked, score between eight and ten.

2. **Personal Space**

   If your horse spooks and runs over you, score between zero and two.

   If when your horse spooks he will do everything to avoid you, you can score between six and eight.

3. **Loading**

   This may not automatically be associated with difficulties with ridden situations, but often the evasions that crop up in loading are also there in the ridden work.

   If your horse is disobedient when loading, score between zero and three.

   If he loads straightaway in a calm and relaxed manner on a loose rope, score between eight and ten.

4. **Schooling**

   If you are working harder than your horse, score below three.

   If your horse works hard for you and shows continual improvement, score eight and above.

5. **Hacking**

   If your horse is very spooky and doesn't listen to you, score below two.

   If your horse is spooky but allows you to control the situation, score more highly.

   It may surprise you that I am not saying horses are not allowed to spook. Horses will spook – they are horses – but when they do, they must still remain under control and listen to you.

Reassess your scores on a regular basis to keep problem areas at the front of your mind and ensure you are making progress, on a monthly basis at the very least. Looking back at old charts, you should be pleasantly surprised to see how your scores improve from the initial benchmark. The reassessment is important so that you can either see the progress you have made and be inspired, or if you aren't making any progress, ask yourself why and change your tactics. If you are following your pyramid plan correctly there should always be progress, no matter how small.

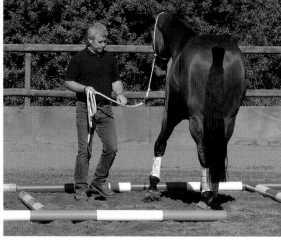

Better brain control

Believe it or not, you can train your horse to deal calmly with new situations. Like everything else, it's a matter of preparation.

By taking your horse through a combined process of desensitization to any frightening stimuli he is likely to encounter, and specific schooling so he is familiar with the job in hand, you can ensure that his left brain is the part in charge on the day.

For example, if you decide that you would like to go to a hunter trial, then hoping that your horse is going to turn up at a strange venue and gallop around a course of fences in a calm, controlled manner is asking a lot. As a sympathetic trainer you want to make doing the right thing easy for your horse, so imagine what he will go through on the day, and practise every element beforehand. This might include being dressed in travel gear, loaded into a horsebox, arriving at a new venue and encountering lots of strange horses and sights. And that's before he's even been asked to perform in these new and strange circumstances.

You also have to think about getting his fitness to the required level, practising various fences and jumping techniques at home, and going cross-country schooling. Even if you have a cross-country course at your yard, this is familiar territory and won't stimulate such an emotional right-brain response as hiring a new course away from home.

If your horse is to gain confidence from you, then you need to be feeling secure too, so always make sure that someone can go with you. Reduce your own stress factor by allowing plenty of time and having the correct equipment with you on the day. A 22-foot line will always come in handy so that if your horse does decide he doesn't like a certain fence you can get off his back and ground train him over the fence. Remember, though, that you can't even begin to think about doing this

> ## BE YOUR HORSE'S LEADER
>
> *Virtually all successful trainers of difficult horses have a few things in common:*
> - *they establish their leadership position;*
> - *they gain the horse's confidence;*
> - *they set up some kind of training regime where the horse has to mentally process the situation and deal with it in ways other than through flight.*

The labyrinth is a great exercise for getting your horse to think logically and for shifting his focus totally on to you. Simply lay out a network of poles on the ground and get him walking through, round and over them in hand; go forwards, backwards and sideways. As he really has to think, he will get endorphic release, which will calm him down.

When he is proficient in hand, try it ridden. Here, we are reversing through the labyrinth, so Jo really has to focus on me. In the smaller photograph I am guiding him with only a neckstrap and my legs.

As well as being fun, the labyrinth challenges the horse thoroughly in both mind and body. It also shows up any weaknesses in your control and co-ordination as a rider/handler.

until your ground training at home is perfect. You don't want a face-to-face challenge in the middle of a cross-country course.

Introducing your horse to anything new or potentially scary requires similar preparation. Hacking out is a common situation where horses play up and get into right-brain flight mode. Just because we enjoy it, we assume that the horse will too, and underestimate the number of new sights and sounds that can actually make it quite an unpleasant experience for him if he is not used to it.

All horses are predisposed to react to sights and sounds, and even the most laid-back family cob is entitled to spook at a bird flying out of the hedge. However, it is not acceptable for a horse to hack out looking for things to spook at, or when he does spook to be completely out of control.

1

2

4

Training the brain

I think it doesn't even cross people's minds that they can do some schooling work at home to help in spooky situations. Yet it is very important to incorporate some kind of desensitization work into your training plan, regardless of the type of horse you have.

The best way is to work with someone else on your yard, so one of you is riding and the other is on the ground to help move things about and for safety. The idea is to create a controlled environment with controlled stimuli to provoke a reaction that can be worked with, without the danger of being on the road with unsympathetic road users. Remember you are trying to provoke a reaction, not terrify the life out of your horse, so don't go at it with too much gusto.

You may be wondering why on earth you would want to get your horse to walk over plastic, but it does have practical uses. You will be amazed at how it changes the horse's mindset and gives him the confidence to tackle other scary situations with confidence (after all, it's not likely you'll expect him to do anything half as scary out on a hack). Not only have they achieved something that is perceived by them as life threatening but their respect for you as a rider and handler will have grown enormously.

1 Start by asking your horse to walk between two plastic coats. The wings help him to focus, but at this stage they should be reasonably far apart.

2 It took Jo a few minutes to accept the situation.

3 Increase the difficulty of what you are asking by moving the wings closer together.

4–7 Jo is so obedient that I can do anything in an arena and he will politely follow or stand and wait, depending on what I have requested.

5

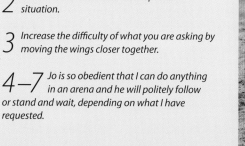

6

3

7

Try an exercise in desensitization

One of the best exercises you can do is to get your horse to walk over a large sheet of plastic. It is easier and fairer to make the sheet as large as possible so that your horse can't just walk round the side of it. It might be advisable to start from the ground.

- Start by asking your horse to back up and come forward off the halter; this is to make sure he is listening to you. Once you have established that he is listening to you, you can then take him to the plastic.

- With your 12-foot rope, position him on one side of the plastic and you on the other, and ask him to come towards you to ease off the pressure. If he starts to move backwards don't pull on the rope. Maintain the same pressure and walk with him until he realizes that walking backwards doesn't gain him anything. He may try you out for a while, so remain calm and keep repeating the question. Remember that just when you are at the point of wanting to give up, the chances are he is too, so just wait. It will be worth it.

- When your horse gives it a go, he might try to jump the plastic sheet with a lot of speed and height, so be aware that this may happen and give him plenty of space and don't get in his way. His reactions will get less each time he does it.

- When he is calmly walking over the sheet you can try the exercise mounted, first with your helper still leading him from the ground, then without. A neckstrap is a good idea when you are in the saddle so that you don't catch your horse in the mouth if he does make any sudden moves. You want to make the experience as pleasant as possible for him.

Once you have achieved this successfully, think of other exercises that will have the effect of challenging your horse's brain, such as filling lots of feed bags with straw and piling them up in the corner, hanging fluorescent jackets on jump wings or getting someone to open an umbrella as he comes past one side of the school. You are teaching your horse to go against his instincts and over-rule the right side of his brain and engage the left, and if you are patient, you will gradually see this happen as he realizes there is nothing to be afraid of and visibly copes better with every pressure.

Focus and attention

The source of many problems is the fact that your horse is not focusing on you.

When I ride and handle my horses I like them to be aware of where I am and what I am doing at all times. Asking for the horse's attention when being trained and ridden is vital if you want your training to be progressive and harmonious. When a horse gives you his attention it shows he is giving you his respect, too. I require a horse's focus when I am trying to teach him something new or improving on what the horse has already learnt, but most of all I need that focus when the situation has the potential to create right-brained behaviour.

A horse's eyes are on the side of their head, so they can look at something on their left with their left eye and the right one won't be able to see it, and vice versa. Thinking of how this affects your horse's life will help you to understand how to deal with ridden issues and to have a better understanding of how your horse ticks.

In order to take control of your horse's mind, you have to have control of his body and vice versa. We have already said that a key stage in the base of your training pyramid is having control over forward, sideways

This little horse has locked one eye and one ear on to the umbrella, showing mild interest, but he is still listening to his rider.

and backward movement in hand. The next stage is to practise getting it under saddle, which is explained in the following chapter. The official name for all that sideways stuff is lateral work, and having a basic knowledge of lateral work is vital, no matter what your chosen discipline.

You may not be interested in dressage tests, but think of all the times you need a well-schooled horse, such as on a hack. To be able to hack safely, you should be able to do turn on the forehand, turn on the quarters, shoulder-in and rein-back (an outline of common lateral exercises and how to do them comes next, in chapter five). Apart from helping you open gates and manoeuvre around obstacles, asking your horse to do this makes him use the left side of his brain, which releases endorphins and could get you out of trouble when hacking.

For example, when hacking out, your horse might catch sight of something on the roadside and want to look at it. He can do one of two things: drop and slightly tilt his head so he can look at it with one eye, showing mild interest without panic, or try to swing his quarters away and at the same time drop and turn his head to look at it with both eyes. By doing this he has turned his total focus towards the perceived problem, and away from you. At this point, getting his focus back will not be at all easy, as he has already started to make 'executive decisions' on what to do next, and your opinion will not be welcomed or even considered at that moment. He has gone right-brained, and his behaviour will be adrenalin-fuelled. Such behaviour is out of your control and thus is frequently frightening and dangerous, which is why it is so important to be able to get and keep your horse's attention. You don't want to get 'blanked out' by your horse when he feels the need to take over.

If you have developed enough control (by practising with those umbrellas and feed bags at home) you will be able to put him into shoulder-in, so that he can't look at the item with two eyes. In my view, the theory about letting a horse have a good look at the object that worries him is misguided; when a horse is allowed to look at a scary object with both eyes it creates adrenalin-fuelled behaviour that makes him difficult to control.

Another good reason for teaching your horse lateral moves is because they help him to develop balance and co-ordination, and ultimately improve his load-carrying capacity and comfort. When it comes to staying calm and in a comfort zone both physically and mentally, a horse has to be balanced and able to carry his own weight easily. An unbalanced horse who finds the displacement of his own weight difficult, never mind that of the rider too, is liable to panic.

Many people misread the signs of an unbalanced horse. When your horse rushes into a fence for example, it's rarely out of excitement because he loves jumping. It's more likely to be because he is unbalanced and worried about the huge task of getting himself and you over the obstacle without losing his feet. The majority of horses I go out to see are totally on their forehand which means that the head, neck and shoulders take most of the weight. This is also why most physiological problems are in these areas and why there are so many riders having schooling and ridden problems with their horses.

Any job you want your horse to do will be affected by his inability to carry and move his own bodyweight easily, and no matter what level you are at, it will prevent you from being progressive in your training.

Who's holding up whom?

Q *I have a lovely horse who is good natured, but hangs off my arms all the time when schooling, unless I let him have a really long rein. I am quite nervous and I think I may be pulling him unintentionally, so he is pulling back. His tack, teeth and back are all fine. How can I learn to trust him and relax?*

Max replies: If you are able to long-line your horse I would start with that. It has two major benefits for you: firstly, the outside line is a constant suggestion that his hocks must come underneath him, which in turn will make him pick up his tummy, round his back and carry himself. The reason he feels like a dead weight is because he is expecting you to carry him, and until his muscles are conditioned it is much easier for him to go about on the forehand with you propping him up.

The easiest way for him to condition himself is without the weight of the rider. Work him for a few weeks on the lines for 20 minutes at a time with lots of upward and downward transitions and changes of direction, with no more than three circuits on one rein before changing, and you will start to see a different horse. After a couple of weeks reduce the amount of time you long-line and start to introduce yourself back on board. You should feel a huge difference.

The second benefit of long-lining is that many of my clients who have lost their nerve find that it helps them regain their confidence and also allows them to see how their horse's work improves and how his shape changes.

Q&A

I travel all over the country, working with horses and riders that span the spectrum of ability and expectation. However, the majority of 'problems' I see share common themes. The queries I have chosen for this section may seem few in number, but I'm prepared to bet you'll find the root of your problem covered by one of them.

This photograph shows how the outside line encourages hock engagement.

Won't go forwards

Q *Earlier this spring I bought a Thoroughbred racehorse off the track in the hope of making him into a dressage horse. He has the looks and movement for the job, and is laid back and very affectionate, but it seems to me that he just does not like to be ridden! He doesn't do anything nasty, he simply stiffens and will not move freely forward.*

I have tried various types of tack and his problem doesn't seem to be anything physical. He moves freely and quite beautifully out in the field, but it's as though he has a mental block when tacked up. I know how to calm a stressed horse, but I don't know how to motivate a seemingly unmotivated horse!

Max replies: First, check to see if he has a problem with his shoulders. I find that many ex-racehorses are jammed up in that area, which doesn't show up as lameness, more as pain from a trapped nerve. You can check this by running your thumb from the centre of the shoulder down through the muscle towards the top of the forearm; if a horse is uncomfortable in this area the muscle will tighten under the pressure of your thumb, and in some cases the horse will show obvious signs of discomfort, such as turning around to have a nip. The muscle should stay relaxed and soft with no tightening. If your horse does show discomfort then get an equine therapist to relieve the pain.

Once you have confirmed that your horse is suffering no physical discomfort, start by ground training with him fully tacked up, but don't tack up in the stable. Instead, take your horse into the school to tack up, and put him on to a 12-foot line and let him work for a while and 'express himself' with the saddle on. Really make him go forwards without worrying about the weight of a rider.

It may be that he hasn't fully accepted the saddle – don't forget that in racing, they don't use a general purpose saddle, so it probably feels a little alien to him. If he wants to have a buck, let him, and once he has calmed down and is going forwards nicely, ask him for a few circuits on each rein and then stop. Ask him to back up and then take him back to his stable or field.

Do this for a few days and see how you get on. If there are no improvements you may be looking at a more serious physiological problem that requires a veterinary consultation.

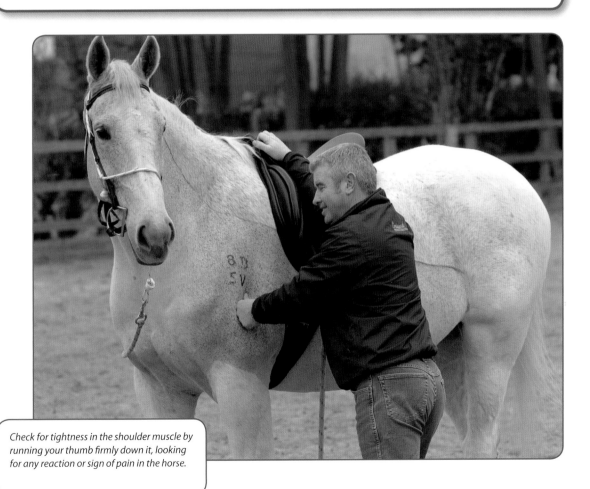

Check for tightness in the shoulder muscle by running your thumb firmly down it, looking for any reaction or sign of pain in the horse.

Q&A

Traffic control

Q *I have a lovely mare who is very good in most ways, apart from when we are on our way home from a hack. She won't stand still at lights or junctions, and won't go forwards, but goes backwards at great speed. It really is frustrating as I don't have any of these problems when schooling her.*

Max replies: If you don't have the universal base of the pyramid in place, great holes will eventually start to appear, and this is a prime example. Sometimes we think our horses are well schooled when in fact all they have done is switch off! They are neither high on adrenalin or calmly endorphic; they are what I term 'in neutral', meaning they don't do much wrong but they don't do much right either.

What your hacking problem has done is to highlight the holes in your training. You are doing

the equivalent of taking out a car with no steering or brakes. Because of the horse's nature, she will favour going right-brained and instinctive in a situation that worries her, which standing at lights or a junction obviously does.

I would forget hacking out for a while and concentrate on putting in place your basic controls, starting with backing up. Make it a discipline so that she can't use it against you. Then test yourself by trying to back up around a circle and a square, which may take a little practice, then finally set out a labyrinth (see pages 114–115) and reverse around that. If doing this from the saddle straightaway is a bit daunting, then start from the ground using a training halter and a 12-foot rope.

When you feel as though you have got more control, do a little of this work before leaving to go on your hack. Five to ten minutes of groundwork beforehand will make the hack a much more pleasurable experience.

Make backing up a discipline and the horse will be less inclined to use it against you. Test yourself by backing up through the labyrinth. Make sure your backing up in hand is perfect before trying it ridden.

Respect is shown in small ways such as the horse standing still for you to mount.

Q&A

Standing to mount

Q *My horse is generally well mannered, except he will not stand close to the block for me to mount. It can take up to half an hour for me to get on. He comes up to the mounting block, but swings his quarters out at the crucial moment. I know this is just naughty behaviour because after a while he gives in and stands like an angel, and then behaves beautifully while being ridden. He also gives in straightaway if I have a helper on the ground.*

Max replies: Mounting problems are surprisingly common and need to be addressed. It really is important that you can mount on your own, as you never know when you will have to.

You say that it can take up to half an hour to get your horse to stand, so what I would like you to do is make good use of that time by putting your horse to work every time he chooses not to let you mount.

Firstly you will need to get yourself a portable mounting block that you can put in your schooling area. Take your horse into the school tacked up but wearing a halter and a 12-foot line.

Present your horse to the mounting block, and if he refuses to stand, send him out on a circle to do a bit of work in trot. After three circuits on each rein bring him back to the mounting block and ask him to stand again. If he does not, then send him away to work again for another three circuits on each rein but this time do two sets of three circuits, so he has done twice as many as last time in total.

Again present him to the mounting block, and every time he doesn't want to stand, send him back out to work and increase the amount of work by either asking for a circuit in canter or an extra circuit. Make the right thing easy and the wrong thing hard work.

It may take you quite a while to get him to stand but he will eventually. Once you are on board let him have a few minutes thinking time in halt, then as hard as it may seem, you need to get off and repeat the exercise several times more. You want him to stand still consistently and reliably when being mounted.

Even if for a week you don't get any riding done, your horse will have exercised himself in mind and body, and the knock-on effect is that you will have built up an enormous amount of respect in other areas that you haven't yet even thought of!

Lazy horse

Q *I have got a very lazy horse who is also a bit big for me. I have to use my leg strongly to get him to move and he always ignores the first kick. I'd like to use just a squeeze, but he doesn't respond, and he also ignores me if I use a whip.*

I hate using a whip or spurs, and don't really like the wip-wop either. I just want him to respond to my leg, so how can I get him more active?

Max replies: If you want to sort this problem out you will have to adopt a positive mindset. Even though you wouldn't normally use a whip or wip-wop (over-and-under, see case study on page 96 for a description), you may have to at first in order to get a result. You have to assess each horse as an individual.

There are two questions I would ask about this horse and his lack of motivation. Firstly, check the physical discomfort theory, as refusing to go forwards is a classic symptom of pain. If everything is fine then you have to ask the question, does my horse respect me? And sadly, in this case, I would have to say that no, he doesn't. It sounds as though he ignores everything you ask.

Get back that respect and sharpen his response times by doing groundwork, long-lining and halter work with lots of direction changes and transitions. Once you have seen an improvement in his response times then get back on board with an over-and-under and ask him to move forwards from your leg. If he doesn't you must use the over-and-under to convey that you say what you mean and mean what you say.

As soon as the horse moves you can quit with the over-and-under, and try some transitions. Ask for an upward transition with your leg, and if nothing happens use the over-and-under. As soon as he changes gear, reward him by quitting the rope, being ready to use it again if he should slow down or stop without being asked.

In my mind it is far more abusive to continually kick your horse to get him to do something. It is much fairer to take a slightly tougher line at first to get him responding to subtle pressure in the long term.

A horse that refuses to go forwards under saddle needs to go back to basics.

Q&A

Hacking excitement

If you must canter, do so alone.

Q *I have recently bought a nine-year-old mare. She is very affectionate, has great stable manners and is good when being ridden in the school. However, when we go on hacks she gets excited and becomes very unpredictable. She will prance about and try to bolt or rear, especially when she thinks we will canter. She sweats up badly and will try anything and everything to get into canter. When we do canter it is very fast and I find it nearly impossible to slow her down. She is worse when she is behind another horse and will always try to overtake. Any suggestions on how I could calm her down?*

Max replies: I would put your horse on a ground-training programme to get her to engage her left brain. It sounds as though her instincts are very close to the surface when hacking, and as we have already discussed, canter is a flight pace in the wild (see page 109). No wonder so many horses find it hard to concentrate on their rider when cantering, especially in a wide open space on a hack.

Ground training will teach her to use the analytical side of her brain, which in turn will stimulate an endorphic release (calming hormones that block the release of adrenalin, the flight hormone). Start the first week by just doing ground training, with lots of changes of direction on either a 12-foot line, or long lines if you feel confident. Use a training halter get her to back up and come forwards, and when you have enough control set out a labyrinth of poles on the ground (see pages 114–115) and get her to back up through the labyrinth. This is an excellent exercise to develop logical left-brain thinking.

Once she is finding this easy, try hacking out again, but do some of these exercises for 15 minutes beforehand to engage her brain, and go back to walk at the first sign of excitement.

Personally, I don't canter my horses in company, as I feel it is asking for trouble of this kind. If I need to do some fast work we go on our own to lessen the adrenalin-fuelled behaviour.

Q&A

Nervous of the leg

Q *My 13hh cob has had a difficult past. I know I ride with my leg too far forwards but when I move it back to where it should be, I feel he is uncomfortable with the pressure as he runs forwards a step or just looks unhappy. When doing groundwork I apply pressure with my hand and he responds well without getting upset. Can you suggest how I can do this when I am riding?*

Max replies: Try not to think about your pony's past. It is sad that he has been abused and it is good that you are sympathetic to his problems, but if you always treat him like an abused horse, he will always behave like one.

With that in mind you must quietly but insistently put your legs where they need to be when riding, just for a few seconds, and then take them off. Keep repeating the process. This repetition is very important if your pony is to learn that he has nothing to fear. Do this exercise while standing with a slightly loose rein and use a neckstrap so that if he does shoot forwards, he doesn't get jabbed in the mouth, and always make sure you are in a safe environment.

Every time he lets you put your legs on, don't forget to take them off and allow him a few seconds thinking time, then reapply them. The few seconds thinking time is like a reward for good behaviour. Once he accepts your leg then you can move on to asking him to move off, and a gentle squeeze should be all that is required.

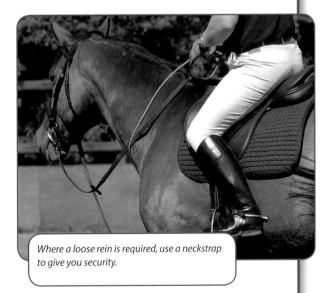

Where a loose rein is required, use a neckstrap to give you security.

Chapter 5

PROGRESS, PROBLEMS AND SOLUTIONS

You are already in possession of the most important tools you need for gaining control of your horse's mind and body: groundwork, and an understanding of how his brain works in training. Now the base of the pyramid is solid, let's get back to the development of strength, balance and co-ordination, which will allow you to refine your work and produce a horse that will do his job well, making your relationship harmonious. However – life is never that simple – this is not about simply showing your horse these processes once and hoping that this will ensure you have that harmonious relationship...Oh no, this is just the beginning. You will have to prove to your horse that you are worthy of your position. He will test your consistency and fairness.

Weight management

Most horses carry around 60 per cent of their weight on the forehand and only 40 per cent on the quarters, so the first step is to redress the balance to 50/50 using the groundwork exercises already described and also the ridden lateral exercises that follow. Only when a horse can carry his own weight should you add the weight of a rider. You can get an indication of the horse's balance by watching where his feet fall when he is in a working pace: in walk the hind feet will overtrack the fore feet, that is they will step in front of the imprints the fore feet have just made; in trot the hind feet will step into the imprints made by the fore feet.

Significant change may take up to three months, so you have to be committed, but the benefits are well worth it in the long term. There is no chance of progressing in your work until this is achieved: it is the stepping stone to the next level.

Jo is balancing himself to execute a turn on the long lines.

Training: Level 2

You may feel that it is not necessary to make these changes because you have no desire to do a dressage test, so why do you need a 'collected' horse? That's like saying that you don't have any intention of wearing a bikini on the beach this summer, so why bother trying to lose weight and going to the gym?

Quite simply, you should lose weight or go to the gym if you need to because it's better for your long-term health and will help your body cope with the stresses and strains of everyday life, no matter what you decide to wear on the beach, and the principle is the same for the horse and his ability to collect.

You owe him the training to develop his strength and carry his body in the most mechanically efficient way, in order to avoid health problems and physical discomfort in his everyday work. It's about developing the horse's core strength, just as an athlete or dancer needs to do. It's no accident that so many horses have problems with their feet and legs at some point in life, particularly the front legs and shoulders. Many of these are associated with the fact that horses are worked on the forehand with their heads held in but their backs hollow and hindquarters not engaged, which is very poor posture for the job they are trying to do. So you may have no interest in competing, but you do have a responsibility to do the best by your horse.

Once your horse is working comfortably at 50/50 then you will be looking to work 40 per cent on the forehand and 60 per cent on the quarters, another big shift for the horse's brain and body.

The horse's ability to carry himself in a shorter frame, and maintain a more upright and powerful posture, is what is described as achieving greater 'collection'. This is a much sought-after state among the dressage fraternity, but also a very useful one for anyone seeking to develop their horse's capacity to carry both his weight and that of a rider with ease and comfort.

Level 2:
Achieving basic control

Key exercises for improvement

In order to achieve control of each of your horse's four limbs or of his quarters (four-directional control, see page 80), you need to have a basic knowledge of lateral work and of how your horse uses his body when carrying out lateral exercises. If your horse doesn't know how to do these exercises, this lack of knowledge will be revealed as huge holes in his abilities at some stage, and will have to be rectified if you want to progress with your training. Lateral exercises can be done from the ground or ridden, although teaching both yourself and your horse from the ground first is the logical place to start. I consider the four basic lateral moves to be as follows:

KEY EXERCISES

1. Rein-back

2. Turn on the forehand

3. Turn on the quarters

4. Shoulder-in

1. Rein-back

It is very important that you can control backward movement in your horse. If you make going backwards a skill or discipline then your horse is less likely to use it as an evasion. It was once thought that asking your horse to go backwards would encourage the evasion, but in fact the opposite is true. Reining back also physically and emotionally asks the horse to back down and become submissive, so it's a very useful 'left-brain' exercise.

Practical uses of rein-back include opening and closing gates out hacking, and being able to back up at a road junction. If your horse decides that he doesn't want to go forwards, putting him in reverse can help with the evasion as you can still insist on going in the direction you want to go, even if it is not in the gear you originally asked for. In a dressage test rein-back is an area in which riders struggle to get good marks, and if you can improve your rein-back to increase your score by just a couple of points it can make all the difference.

To go backwards both you and your horse need to be able to work without adrenalin. When your horse understands how to back up softly from a gentle ask, then you can start to practise backing up in a particular direction. Asking a horse to back up to the left or the right is a bit like trying to reverse a car with a trailer attached, you need to do just the opposite of what you feel you want to do. One of the best ways to practise is to position poles or cones in a school and reverse around them. Keep the work calm and efficient. Never be harsh and never use rein-back as a punishment.

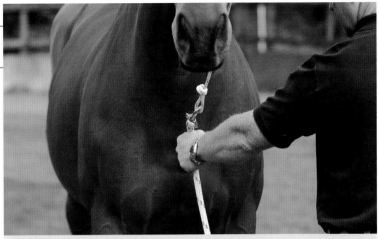

Point your hand at the horse's chest to get a straight rein-back.

To send the horse's quarters to the right when backing, you need to ask for rein-back with your hand out past his left shoulder.

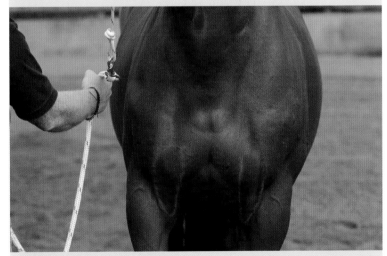

Put your hand out beside the right shoulder to move the horse's quarters to the left when backing. If your horse reins-back to one side, you may be inadvertently asking him to bend. Check your hand position.

Rein-back in hand

Stand and face your horse, with the rope in your left hand and the coils in the right, with the fingers of your left hand uppermost. Advance to your horse with his head on the outside of your left hand. Exert mild pressure on his nose and wait for a response. You want your horse to move all four feet backwards, just one step. Once they have done this, relax and wait several seconds before asking again – remember the Four Rs (page 58).

If your horse is adamant that he is not going to back up, do not simply apply more pressure. He is trying to draw you into a physical match that he will win. Instead, try sending him away on the 12-foot rope for three circuits of a circle. Then, ask him to come back, stop, relax and ask again. You know your horse and have to decide what is the correct amount of pressure and what is too much. If he refuses again, send him away to work again. Remember this is not to tire your horse, but to get him to realize there is a consequence to saying no to your polite request. When he does make a step backwards make a huge fuss of him and then repeat the request. It won't take long for him to realize that doing the right thing is easy and the wrong thing is more difficult.

Another tactic is to move to the side of the horse and ask him to move his quarters over, as in turn on the forehand. Do this on both reins and then ask him to back up again. This exercise takes control of the brakes by freeing up the quarters.

Repeat the backing-up work until your horse can do it really nicely. This is not a try-again-tomorrow issue, you need to stick it out until your horse can repeat it softly and easily.

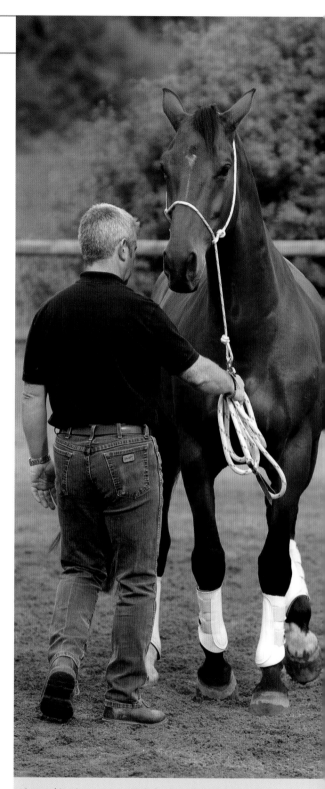

I am asking Jo to move straight backwards. This is not an easy task for any horse, as they really have to think about where they are putting their feet. Look at Jo's ears: they show that he is concentrating hard on where his quarters are going.

Once your horse is listening to you then you can ask for more advanced backing up which is with visual pressure only, for example with a wiggle of the rope or you walking into his personal space. To execute a good rein-back under saddle it is important to get the rein-back on the ground perfect first.

Jo moving backwards from visual pressure created by a rhythmic wiggling of the rope (above). One of the by-products of teaching a horse to back is that he gains respect for personal space. Remember to keep your feet still and have relaxed body language when doing this exercise (below).

Rein-back ridden

Do not attempt rein-back in the saddle if your groundwork isn't excellent. We want to make life easier for the horse, not for him to view rein-back as a punishment. It is another tool in the box that can only be used effectively for problem solving when the horse is good at it.

Jo under saddle performing rein-back. Notice the back lifts and the head stays still, which should also happen in hand.

Start by sitting squarely in the saddle. Take an even contact equally on both reins while raising your hands slightly, to give the horse an 'upward' feel so that he doesn't think you are pulling him backwards. Next, gently but rhythmically use both legs at the same time, using pressure and release, in good steady rhythm. It may take a few seconds for your horse to work out what you are asking for, so don't be in a hurry to increase the pressure. If you do have to increase the pressure then do so evenly with hands and legs, and again wait for a response. Once the horse has moved all his feet backwards, soften your hands and stop the on/off pressure of your legs and let your horse think about what has just happened.

When you ask for rein-back again, go back to using minimum pressure and only increase the pressure if you have to. Remember we want more for doing less. Keep practising. When your horse starts to get quicker and more fluid you will achieve a true two-time movement. This exercise will give you greater flexion at the poll, lift the horse's back and help towards your collection work, if that's what you want to do, or just help with simple tasks such as opening and closing gates when mounted. Never use backing up as a punishment, especially from the saddle.

KEY EXERCISE

2. Turn on the forehand

Most of a horse's evasions are achieved using either the quarters or the shoulders, so being able to control these areas is very important. I find that around 20 per cent of all evasions are through the quarters, while 80 per cent occur through the shoulders.

When your horse turns on the forehand, he is moving his hindquarters. By pushing his hindlegs across and underneath his body, the horse will become stronger through the quarters and behind the saddle, encouraging correct posture and helping to avoid future back problems. Turn on the forehand will also help your horse to engage from behind – the start of self-carriage (see page 145).

From a safety point of view, if you have the ability to control the quarters you have a better chance of being able to cancel out behaviour such as bucking and rearing if necessary: a horse has to be able to firmly plant his feet to execute these evasions and you have learnt how to disengage them. You will also be able to open and close gates out hacking and prevent your horse swinging his quarters dangerously into traffic, for example.

From a schooling point of view, controlling the quarters enables the rider to prevent them from swinging out or in, and it will help strengthen and create suppleness behind the saddle enabling the hindlegs to cover more ground, which will lead to better engagement.

Practising without realizing it when working on the yard!

Turn on the forehand in hand

Face your horse, then move quietly down the nearside with about 45cm (18in) between your side and his. Once you draw level with the driving line (see page 80), you can spin the end of your rope, or put your hand out to drive the quarters away from you. Your left hand needs to be about 15–20cm (6–8in) from the clip of the rope, to stop your horse walking away in a straight line.

As the quarters start to move away from you, you need to do a half turn through your own body so that your chest faces the horse's hip, which gives you a very strong driving position. The idea is to get your horse to step the hindleg nearest you as far across the path of the other hindleg as he can, making sure that the step is inside the opposite hindleg, not outside.

This exercise must be repeated on both reins until your horse is moving at your slightest requests.

Turn on the forehand ridden

When turning to the right, the quarters move to the left and there needs to be a direct relationship between your right leg and the right hind, so when you ask it to move over it does so instantly.

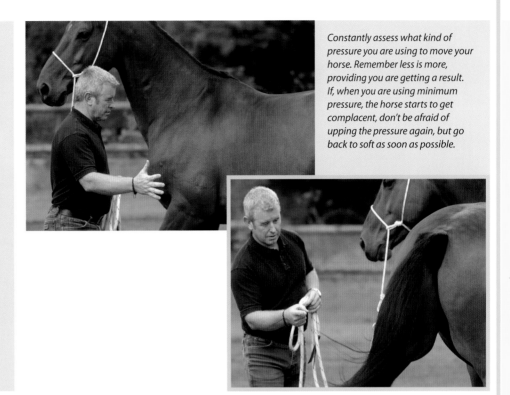

Jo is being asked to move his hindquarters around his forehand in hand. He is a supple horse and this shows the amount of stepping over that can be achieved. If a horse can step over this far he will be able to engage further underneath himself. Also when the leg is travelling this way nearly all forward drive is lost, which will enable you to stop your horse better and improve on downward transitions.

Constantly assess what kind of pressure you are using to move your horse. Remember less is more, providing you are getting a result. If, when you are using minimum pressure, the horse starts to get complacent, don't be afraid of upping the pressure again, but go back to soft as soon as possible.

Sit squarely in the saddle and relax. To turn to the right, the horse's quarters need to move to the left. Flex your horse's head to the right gently until you can see the corner of his right eye. Use the left rein to support the bend, with enough contact to stop your horse from walking forwards, but without pulling backwards. Now take your right leg and place it about 15cm (6in) behind your normal leg position (this distance will lessen as your horse becomes more familiar with the movement) and apply it on the horse's side. Wait for a response; if the response is poor don't use more leg but bend the neck a bit further and wait, without taking your leg off.

Each time you have to wait for a response, allow your horse several seconds thinking time before increasing the bend in the neck. It is better in the early stages to use more bend than more leg to get a result, as you don't want to dull your horse's response to the leg. This needs to be repeated on both reins until the movement is slick.

KEY EXERCISE

3. | Turn on the quarters

Turn on the quarters gives the control of the forehand which is where 80 per cent of all evasions occur especially the more serious ones, such as napping, spooking, running out at fences, rearing and spinning.

Turn on the quarters frees up the shoulder and displaces the weight to the hindquarters. The ability to do this movement effectively is the linchpin in dealing with crookedness and many other related schooling problems, such as falling in or out, and incorrect canter leads.

In hand

Being able to achieve turn on the quarters gives you control of 80 per cent of the horse. This makes this exercise a really tough question for your horse, as such huge amounts of control are psychologically difficult for a horse to accept. In turn, this means it will really start to cement your relationship with him, in both ridden and handling situations.

Stand facing your horse's neck and shoulders on the near side. Put your left hand on your horse's face around the noseband of the halter, and put your right hand on his shoulder. Slightly encourage your horse to take a quiet step forwards and when he lifts the leg nearest to you gently but firmly push him off the ground away from you. This should cause him to place his left foreleg across the path of the right foreleg. Then stop, relax and praise.

Once you can do this a step at a time easily, try for two steps then three, and eventually aim to keep going until you have turned a full circle around the quarters. This will be a challenge at first as it will show up any lack of dexterity and suppleness in both you and the horse. It must be perfect in both directions before you try it from the saddle.

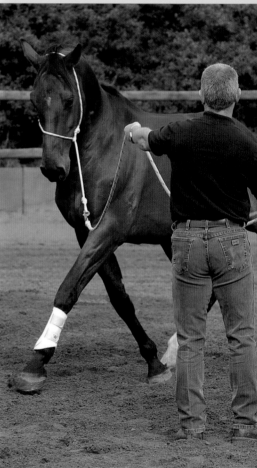

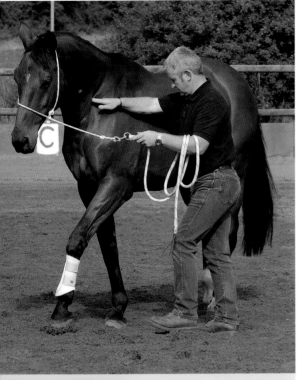

Ridden

When moving to the right, sit square and relaxed in the saddle, and flex the horse's neck to the right in exactly the same way as for turn on the forehand. The difference now is to open the right rein (take it away from the horse's neck) and close the left rein. Place the rein on the horse's neck, as if you are leading with the right rein and driving with the left. Now open the right leg (relax it or slightly take it away from the horse's side), and with your left leg on the girth, apply a firm but consistent pressure. This is the moment when you know if you have done enough work in hand or not.

With this exercise your objective is to get your horse to place his weight on to the right leg to allow the left leg to be picked up and placed across and in front of the right. Repeat on both reins until perfect, but don't fall into the trap of using lots of pressure to get a little response.

Now that you have both of these exercises perfect in both directions from the ground and in the saddle you have totally changed the dynamic between you and your horse. You have taught him that your leg doesn't just mean forwards but also sideways, which will help you in many situations.

Jo has advanced beyond the point where I need to put a hand on his face to ask for the turn. Here he starts stepping round from a touch on the shoulder and direction from my body language (above). In the early stages, you will find that progress will be one step at a time, and you really have to be aware of allowing the horse thinking time.

Jo is now moving through the shoulders away from visual pressure. Although this isn't a perfect movement, it shows how little pressure you need to move a shoulder. This work will make it much easier for your horse to respond to your requests when you are riding.

Being able to pick up and move the horse's shoulders on the ground and in the saddle improves your steering, helps to move his weight back towards his quarters, and gives you more control of both his physical and his emotional sides.

KEY EXERCISE

4. Shoulder-in

Shoulder-in builds up engagement of the quarters and frees the shoulders to enable the rider to have more control. It is one of the most influential movements for suppling the horse.

From a practical point of view, it is probably the best tool to have in your box for horses who don't like to go past spooky objects out on a hack, and is fabulous for dustbin days! Instead of letting your horse look at the object and get spooky, put him into shoulder-in and don't let him look or even think about it. As I said earlier, I am not a fan of the 'let him get a good look at it' school of thought. I do not believe in allowing horses to focus on things that are frightening them.

In hand

Start from the ground, as not only will this help your horse understand what is expected from him when you want to do it from the saddle, but it also helps your relationship with your horse by showing him how many different ways you can move him around, and not vice versa. It is a stepping stone towards shoulder-in under saddle, especially if your horse hasn't done it before, or has started to become difficult about moving both forwards and sideways at the same time.

When you first start working on shoulder-in, use a fence line to work down as this will help you to control the forward movement, and is like having an extra pair of hands to assist. So start with your horse facing the fence at a 45-degree angle slightly looking in the direction you are about to go. Put one hand on the halter and the other on the horse's shoulder, and taking one step at a time move your horse down the fence line. (Remember, to achieve this you will have to be proficient at turn on the quarters and around the forehand, otherwise it will not make sense to your horse and he won't understand what you are asking of him.) Repeat both each ways until you and your horse are finding this quite easy.

If you find that your horse is reluctant to move his shoulders, go back to turn on the quarters in hand to re-establish control of the shoulders. The angle in hand is quite a steep angle to move laterally, but for training purposes it helps to emphasize the angle and will make ridden shoulder-in a great deal easier, as you will use less of an angle.

Shoulder-in, in hand is best executed along a fence to start with as this will help you to get sideways movement without the horse walking forwards. Always check your own position when asking your horse to move over. You will find that you need to be between the head and the shoulder to get the best movement.

Ridden

Once you can easily move your horse along the fence line both ways in hand, it is time to try shoulder-in ridden. You may want to continue using the fence line as you did when in hand, with your horse's start position the same, but instead of your hands pushing the horse, it is your leg and rein doing the pushing.

So to move to the right, place more weight onto your left seatbone and close the left leg and hand to create flexion to the left. The left leg then pushes the horse sideways, while the right leg stays relaxed and slightly drawn back to control the horse's quarters. The right rein is used to control your horse's forward movement.

In the beginning, don't aim to do shoulder-in all the way down the fence line. Establish each step, one at a time, and look for quality not quantity. Once you are comfortable doing this both ways, move away from the fence and face the opposite way to do the exercise, that is, look towards the middle of the school. Your aids will be exactly the same.

If you are aiming for a safe and pleasant hack, then you should now be able to do that: you will have achieved your goal.

HALT!

Although not a lateral move, another important exercise to teach your horse is to halt and stand. It is totally irresponsible as a driver to go out on the roads when your car handbrake doesn't work, yet a horse jigging about at a road junction is a fairly common sight. The ability to be still shows a horse's readiness to be patient and quiet. In my experience, horses that can stand are generally a pleasure to be around.

Troubleshooting:
Lateral work

1. Crooked

If I had a horse that was crooked in canter when going to the right on the right rein, I would have to assume that there was a stiffness in that bend, and would over-correct in walk and trot first. Remember when I talked about left- and right-brain thinking (pages 104–107), horses find it easier to stay calm and think clearly in these two paces (page 109).

When I say over-correct I mean instead of just trying to correct the horse's neck back to the centre, I would over-correct it to the left. By doing this you will be stretching the side that is tight so that when you ask for canter you will be more likely to start to get a straighter canter. It might only be for a few strides, but if you do this every time you school, you will soon find you don't need to correct at all. If your horse's problems are on the other rein then over-correct to the right.

Turn on the quarters helps straightness. You can see that Ferdi is lifting his off fore and bringing it across. This teaches him that you can control his shoulders on the move (see page 118).

2. One-sided

Once a horse goes better on one rein than the other, the temptation is to work him more on the 'bad' rein, but that is only going to keep reminding him that he is not comfortable on that rein. Again lots of groundwork is useful, but also try this ridden exercise.

On the rein that is stiff, walk for one circuit, then ask your horse to turn on to his good rein and trot or canter for a few circuits – no more than three as most horses will switch off after this. Then go back to the stiff rein and walk again for one circuit, and keep repeating this until your horse offers you more by his choice on the stiff rein because going on the other rein is proving to be hard work. It is all a bluff, but it will get your horse to choose to go on his stiff rein, rather like making someone think that a good idea was theirs in the first place!

A word on correction

After all this planning and preparation, you may now be disappointed if your horse doesn't get it all absolutely right first time. Of course, he won't! Practice is the key, but remember it is only *perfect* practice that makes perfect. You still need to abide by the training rules.

For a long time I thought the way to correct horses was to prevent the behaviour I didn't want from happening in the first place, but now I realize it's a more useful training exercise to allow that behaviour, and then correct it. Otherwise, how does the horse know when he has done something wrong?

When you are correcting a horse, you are not trying to dominate him, but to modify the movement or posture while making sure your horse doesn't perceive your correction as punishment, as this will only hamper your schooling and training.

When I think of 'correction', it is in terms of ensuring that the problem is no longer there, rather than simply masking or avoiding it by constantly using my hands or my legs to stop the horse going wrong for example. It's about putting the responsibility back on to the horse for carrying himself, and a huge percentage of this can be corrected through halter training and long-lining.

If you are wasting a lot of valuable time going over and over the same correction, stop telling yourself that one day it will come right. Clearly, the horse hasn't worked out what you want for some reason, or has worked it out but chosen not to carry it out, so get to the bottom of why.

A common reason is that the horse is used to being micro-managed by the rider and hasn't learned to take responsibility for any of his work or to self-motivate.

Again, ground training and consistently sticking to the Four Rs (see page 58) is the answer. But don't mistake a lack of physical strength for a lack of co-operation. Initially, the likelihood is that your horse will only be physically able to maintain the correction for a few seconds before reverting back to his old way of going, but you have to use this as a base to work from. Each time you ask, the period of correction will get longer until your horse is going in a correct way without you asking.

Level 3:
Aiming for the top

All horses benefit from being trained in the five skills that are vital for the competition horse. These produce a horse that is willing and capable of doing all that you ask, softly and responsively, whether on a hack around the block, over a taxing show-jumping or cross-country course or in a difficult dressage test.

KEY SKILLS

1. Suppleness

Suppleness is the antidote to tension and comes from working through the groundwork and ridden exercises specified in the base levels of the pyramid. It is the main requirement for a relaxed and co-ordinated horse as it allows all the muscles and joints to work in unison. In order for the horse to be supple, he needs to be relaxed, and vice versa.

2. Rhythm

Working with suppleness allows you to start to develop your horse's rhythm. Rhythm is of major importance to make the best of your horse's ability, regardless of the level you are at, or the discipline you choose. Being aware of rhythm helps your horse to become more balanced; while working rhythmically has a metronome-like effect on his brain and is a calming influence, so he will find it easier to remain relaxed, especially when away from home.

3. Engagement

The nice thing about breaking things down and working on them piece by piece is that it allows you to perfect them as you go. Once your primary objectives have been achieved, you will start to see the knock-on effects, and realize that focusing on the small things will improve the bigger picture.

Achieving suppleness and rhythm will give you engagement, which is essential for progressive training. Engagement refers to the horse's ability to transfer weight on to his quarters and lower the hocks for greater 'spring', control and weight-bearing ability, rather than propping himself up with his forehand. Engagement is crucial for the horse to be able to maintain correct posture and to carry his weight and that of the rider with ease and beauty.

4. Straightness

Straightness can only come after suppleness, rhythm and engagement. I feel horses are asked to be straight long before they are ready or have the necessary skills.

Not being straight is one of the main problems to affect training and is a major factor in problems such as rearing, bucking and spooking. Nearly all the ridden problems I see come from crooked horses; it is no wonder they can't cope with more advanced forms of training. A lack of straightness is a major cause of evasive patterns developing in horses including leading, loading and handling.

5. Self-carriage

This is the holy grail of riding and training and is a by-product of suppleness, rhythm, engagement and straightness. It is the last piece of the puzzle and is only achieved when the other parts are in place. A lot of horses don't work well because the rider is trying to achieve self-carriage first, rather than wait until it comes as a result of correct and progressive training. Pushing the horse to carry himself beyond his limits too soon is the quickest way to stop him going forwards. He will look for every excuse not to work for you.

I prefer the term 'self-carriage' to 'on the bit' as I feel the latter phrase can encourage people to focus on the bit for all the wrong reasons. Starting with the bit and working backwards (rather than focusing on the quarters' carrying capacity and working forwards) is not the way to get the horse to work in the correct outline, and will impede progress and development.

Self-carriage can only be achieved if the horse is supple, can work straight, in rhythm and with engagement. There are no shortcuts.

Level 4:
Stepping up to the challenge

All too often horses are asked to produce their best performance without having all the skills to give it. The pyramid (see pages 34–5) is a visual tool to show you what goes into training a horse to be polite, relaxed, obedient, and eventually, if required, to be able to perform at competitions. You and your horse can only make progress if you work at each level in turn, ensuring your skills are complete before moving on to the next level. There is nothing to be gaining by rushing through the pyramid, trying to get to the top as quickly as possible. This is simply going through the motions and your horse has no hope of being able to achieve his full potential if he is not given a chance to learn each skill thoroughly and be comfortable with it before moving on to the next. Once you have worked through levels 1, 2 and 3, you are well on the way to stepping up to the challenge of using what you have taught your horse to achieve your goal, whatever that might be.

KEY SKILLS

1. Half-halt

Half-halt is a simple form of pressure and release and has a huge number of benefits. It momentarily engages the horse's brain and body to prepare for transitions, and also improves collection and your horse's outline. It also gives you the ability to slow down the pace to regain either the horse's outline or give additional control.

2. Shortening and lengthening

Being able to shorten and lengthen your horse's stride is a good gauge of your control over movement, particularly in transitions. Often horses are only worked in one outline and frame, but using these tools will bring many benefits and variation to your schooling programme.

Your horse will grow and develop better muscles in the right places to enable him to carry himself better and to maintain correct posture in all paces and directions. He will be better able to respond to your requests without losing rhythm and engagement and thus will become more gymnastic.

3. Paces within a pace

Being able to lengthen and shorten will lead you to working on 'paces within a pace', a further refinement. For example, lengthening the stride is not a matter of quickening the pace. Paces within a pace are a test of the carrying capacity of the horse's quarters as well as his straightness, suppleness, rhythm and self-carriage.

Mattie is showing good engagement which enables him to really stretch his frame, resulting in expressive extensions and easy transitions between the paces.

The Pinnacle
Reaching the top

For a lot of people, reaching the top is not about competing but about their relationship with their horse, and by improving your relationship through this work you will be able to ask more of your horse while still being fair and not losing his confidence in you when out hacking. For those people who want to compete, it is fascinating that these methods really can improve the competition horse in all disciplines, including racing. Many people see competing as loading difficult horses into lorries and trailers and hoping that they will behave at the other end, but there is far more to it than just that – proper preparation can and does produce more chances of success.

For a long time, I have felt isolated in my belief that these methods provide a better way of training. However, more recently my work has become far more widely accepted as normal and useful. I didn't start out to be different from everyone else, I just wanted to be more effective as a horseman and to keep learning, and I believe that this has enhanced my work.

A horse with a great mindset is easy to train and a joy to have around the yard. Spread the Word (Fly) is proof of that: we bred him and established firm foundations early on, as a result, when his new owners took him on, they found him very easy to train.

Fly is now eventing at intermediate level and is doing very well.

The Pinnacle

A final word on
problem solving

When it comes to schooling and improving our horses, there is an almost endless number of problems and things we'd like to change. I planned to address the most common in this book. I was all set to come up with my solutions for problems such as hurrying into transitions, falling out of transitions, horse not going forwards, horse too keen to go forwards, horse hanging on the rider's hands, throwing head in canter, sticking his tongue out…. The list seems endless, but when I started to think about each one individually, I realized that the answer to all of them was pretty much the same.

I have had to deal with many problems over the years and through trial and error I have found that going through all the groundwork exercises in a huge percentage of horses will sort out all of the above areas.

Many of you will be familiar with my old horse Pelo (pictured, right) who featured quite a lot in demonstrations and previous books. When I first got him I became very frustrated that I wasn't getting anywhere with his ridden work. He had been abused previously and wasn't prepared to give in easily; he would even throw himself on the floor if pushed. I was at my wits' end so I got off his back and spent three months training him from the ground. With loads of halter work and long-lining, our relationship improved and he became a real star at doing it all. When I got back on, he was engaged, forward-going and ready to listen to me, yet he kept his very cheeky personality. I was then able to train him.

Until that point, although I had always used some kind of groundwork, I hadn't realized its relevance in solving schooling problems. The thing about groundwork is that the areas you have problems with are probably the areas that are also your ridden problems, so for example your circling work will help you with control of each separate quarter and gives you the ability to disengage as well as engage the hindquarters.

Start to think of problems as part of a whole, and read what they tell you about your relationship with your horse and the gaps in your current training regime, rather than looking at each one in isolation.

Useful Addresses

Richard Maxwell
c/o Equestrian Services Ltd
46 Ruffles Road
Haverhill
Suffolk   CB9 0JX
Tel: (01440) 702327
e-mail: equestservices@toucansurf.com
www.richard-maxwell.com
Website designed by www.compuplan.co.uk

Equissage
Tel: (0800) 072 1180
e-mail: info@equissage.co.uk
www.equissage.co.uk

Jump 4 Joy
Knowles Fields Industrial Estate
Alcester Road
Inkberrow
Worcestershire   WR7 4HR
Tel: (01386) 793339
Fax: (01386) 792030
e-mail: info@jump4joy.co.uk
www.jump4joy.co.uk

Performance Patches
c/o Equestrian Merchandise Ltd
14 Woodyard Close
Brigstock
Northants   NN14 3LZ
Tel: (01536) 373049
e-mail: jan.banham@virgin.net
www.performancepatches.co.uk

Brook Farm Equestrian Centre and Livery Yard
Hempstead Road
Radwinter
Saffron Walden
Essex   CB10 2TH
Tel: (01799) 599262

Long-lining teaches your horse to carry himself, and the line behind the hocks is a constant suggestion to him to put his hocks further underneath him, which creates engagement. The horse becomes straighter and more forward in his transitions both upwards and downwards, and learns greater balance through transitions and turns.

I truly believe that no matter what your problem is, by doing the work suggested in this book you will see far more of an improvement than doing more of the same troubleshooting.

Index